"I stood tall as I heard the first Craft ~~~~ ~~~~ ~~~~ carefully chosen being called ~~~~ ~~~~ ~~~~ the sheet was ripped from my ~~~~ in the robe I had made for the ~~~~

"The high priest and priest~~~~ ~~~~ me. Then they took my measu~~~~ ~~~~ a white cord to my exact height. I would wear this cord as long as I was a part of the coven, a symbolic umbilical cord linking me to my brothers and sisters in the Craft.

"I felt like a new person—I felt like a Witch."

Drawing from more than 15 years of experience as a Witch, Edain McCoy opens the world of covens to solitary Witches everywhere. This book will answer all of your questions about joining a coven:

- Where do I find networking resources?
- How will I know which coven is right for me?
- What happens at a coven initiation?
- What precautions should I take when meeting with strangers in a prospective coven?
- How can I create a coven or study circle from scratch?
- What are the inner circle secrets that covens vow to keep to themselves?
- How do covens do magick and healing?

If you're already in a coven, your group will find all sorts of helpful advice in this book, including:

- How can we screen potential coven members?
- What can we do when leadership goes sour?
- What's an effective ritual for banishing a coven member?
- What kills covens?

About the Author

Edain McCoy became a self-initiated Witch in 1981, and has been an active part of the Pagan community since her formal initiation into a large San Antonio coven in 1983. She has been researching alternative spiritualities since her teens, when she was first introduced to Kaballah (Jewish mysticism). Today she is a part of the Wittan Irish Pagan Tradition and a Priestess of Brighid within that tradition. A descendant of the infamous feuding McCoy family of Kentucky, Edain also proudly claims as a forefather Sir Roger Williams, the seventeenth century religious dissenter.

To Write to the Author

If you wish to contact the author or would like more information about this book, please write to the author in care of Llewellyn Worldwide, and we will forward your request. Both the author and publisher appreciate hearing from you. Llewellyn Worldwide cannot guarantee that every letter written to the author can be answered, but all will be forwarded. Please write to:

Edain McCoy
℅ Llewellyn Worldwide
P.O. Box 64383, Dept. K666-1
St. Paul, MN 55164-0383, U.S.A.

Please enclose a self-addressed, stamped envelope for reply, or $1.00 to cover costs. If outside the U.S.A., enclose international postal reply coupon.

THE WITCH'S
COVEN

Finding
or
Forming
Your Own
Circle

EDAIN MCCOY

2003
Llewellyn Publications
St. Paul, Minnesota 55164-0383
U.S. A.

Cover design: Gavin Dayton Duffy
Cover leaf and ivy images photos © Photodisc
Editing and layout: Marguerite Krause
Book design and project management: Amy Rost

SECOND EDITION
First printing, 2003
(previously titled *Inside A Witches' Coven*, four printings, 1999)

ISBN: 0-7387-0388-5, Cataloging-in Publication data under former ISBN:
Library of Congress Cataloging-in Publication Data
McCoy, Edain, 1957–
     Inside a witches' coven/Edain McCoy — 1st ed.
        p. cm. — (Llewellyn's modern witchcraft series)
     Includes index.
     ISBN 1-56718-666-1
        1. Witchcraft. 2. Covens   I. Title. II. Series
     BF1572.C68M37   1997
     133.4'3—dc21

     Llewellyn Worldwide does not participate in, endorse, or have any authority or responsibility concerning private business transactions between our authors and the public. All mail addressed to the author is forwarded but the publisher cannot, unless specifically instructed by the author, give out an address or phone number.
     Any Internet references or company addresses contained in this work are current at publication time, but the publisher cannot guarantee that a specific location will continue to be maintained. Please refer to the publisher's website for links to authors' websites and other sources.

Llewellyn Publications
A Division of Llewellyn Worldwide, Ltd.
P.O. Box 64383
St. Paul, Minnesota 55164-0383
www.llewellyn.com

Printed in the United States of America

Other Books by Edain McCoy

Witta: An Irish Pagan Tradition

A Witch's Guide to Faery Folk: Reclaiming Our Working Relationships With Invisible Helpers

How to Do Automatic Writing

Celtic Myth & Magick: Harness the Power of the Gods and Goddesses

The Sabbats: A New Approach to Living the Old Ways

Mountain Magick

Lady of the Night: A Handbook of Moon Magick & Rituals

Entering the Summerland: Customs and Rituals of Transition into the Afterlife

Making Magick

Celtic Women's Mysteries

Astral Projection for Beginners

Spellworking for Covens

Contents

10 Teaching Secrets and Secret Teachings 155

The rewards and frustrations of being part of a teaching coven—How we organized our teaching circle—Keeping an up-to-date teaching chart—Other ways to structure a teaching coven—The teaching experience—Those folks you should probably not teach—The veiled workings of the inner-circle—Traditional reasons that covens kept secrets—What types of secrets were and are kept by covens

11 Resolving Conflicts and Parting Ways 171

The drawbacks of having no governing authority—Why individuals might leave covens—The life expectancy of the average coven—What kills covens—Ideas for parting rituals—Ideas for rituals marking an end to a coven—Creative problem solving—Compacts, mediators, and heroic efforts—Reasons for banishment—Methods of banishment

Chapter 1

WELCOME
to the WORLD of the
WITCH'S COVEN

THE CIRCLE HAD ALREADY BEEN CAST when Sheva, Jason, and I were led by a candlelight procession of elders into its center. The high priestess closed the gateway behind us with her ritual knife, separating us in time and space from the mundane world. The light of the full moon shone softly on our ritual knoll in the rugged Texas Hill Country, the soft glow of dozens of white candles making the scrub oaks and bermuda grass appear like an enchanted forest surrounding us with its protecting love. I was tingling with anticipation, trying to remain serious when all I wanted to do was dance with excitement. The high priest and priestess stood before us, seeming to sense this barely contained force, and they smiled warmly as they touched my forehead in blessing.

Beside me stood Sheva, who amazed me with her apparent composure. She and I had been friends for a long time. We had become interested in Witchcraft together, and had undergone self-initiations two years earlier. Now we stood with another newcomer, Jason, all of us wrapped in black sheets awaiting our official initiation into the Craft. When the night ended we would not only be fully initiated Witches, but sworn members of a coven, part of a spiritual family.

Forty loving faces stood in the shadowy reaches of the circle's perimeter, forty people who had taught us, nurtured us, and helped us to reach this night. The flowery words spoken by the high priest and priestess, and my responses to them, only vaguely registered in my mind. I remember drinking honey ale from a silver cup, being touched on my shoulders, head, and feet by the edge of a ritual blade, and then being asked to kneel in a fetal position, drawing the black sheet up over my head.

As the three of us remained squatting on the ground, each alone under his/her own dark sheet, I wondered where this decision to become a Witch would eventually lead. I knew I had no doubts that this was the spiritual path for me, and I was overjoyed at having found a coven whose members had welcomed me into their family. It seemed as if my world of possibilities had no limits.

Shrouded in black, I sensed rather than saw the initiation rite continuing around me. Occasionally I heard salted water spatter against my covering, or felt the tip of a blade on my head. All the while I stayed crouched like an infant awaiting my birth.

Then, through the darkness, I heard a disembodied voice at my ear asking me to reaffirm my wish to be initiated. Did I know what it meant to be a Witch? Did I know what it meant to take this final step? Was I prepared both mentally and spiritually for its challenges? Did I love the God? Would I serve the Goddess?

Just as I was beginning to break out in a nervous sweat, the high priest cried in a joyful voice, "Arise, sister Shira, and be reborn into the family of the Goddess."

I stood tall as I heard the first Craft name I had so carefully chosen being called aloud for the first time. As I arose, the sheet was ripped from my head, leaving me standing proudly in the forest-green robe I had made for the occasion. The high priest and priestess kissed my cheeks and hugged me. Then they took my measure by cutting a white cord to my exact height. I would wear this cord as long as I was a part of the coven, a symbolic umbilical cord linking me to my brothers and sisters in the Craft.

When Sheva and Jason were also standing in their new robes, wearing their new cords, we walked clockwise around the circle lighting candles held by each covenor, the passing of the flames a symbol of our unity. To each person in the circle we repeated a simple statement of allegiance to the coven. We promised our perfect love and perfect trust. Then we each went to the altar and pledged our faith and honor to our deities.

Still starry-eyed, we took our places along the outer edge of the circle with the others. Our esbat, or full moon, ritual was about to begin, with us—the three newest members of the coven—ready and eager to fully participate. I felt like a new person—I felt like a Witch.

What It's Like to Be in a Coven

The oldest spiritual practices on the planet are now some of today's fastest-growing religious movements, attracting an increasing number of people of all ages, all income levels, all ethnic backgrounds, and all political and sexual orientations. In spite of our diversity, what we all have in common is a desire to reconnect with Mother Earth, and to worship her as a divine entity the way our ancestors did thousands of years ago. We also have a common need to reach out to, and connect with, like-minded persons for worship, study, and mutual support. To this end we form or join covens.

"Coven" is one of the names used to define a cohesive group of Witches who work and worship together on a regular basis. The word *coven* comes from the same root as the modern English word *convene,* meaning "to come together." Other terms synonymous with *coven* are *grove, sept, touta, clan,* and *cove.*

Covens come in all sizes and structures, many of them good, some mediocre. A few could possibly be called dangerous. A coven may have only two members; I have known others containing as many as sixty. There are almost as many different types of covens as there are Witches, and certainly there are at least as many different ways to run a coven as there are individual Craft traditions. Though there are strong central tendencies and common practices to be found, variations on the theme are legion. This small book cannot hope to examine all the many ways in which an individual coven might interpret its festivals, rites of passage, internal structures, or magickal practices. I do not, and would not try, to speak for all Witches.

This book explores those central tendencies through examples of covens I have been a part of, have known about, or with which I have worked and worshiped.

Finding, developing, and worshiping in a coven with other Witches is not always the ideal experience Craft lore and some Craft books lead us to believe. This is not to say that it can't be, or that it shouldn't be. Many of us have been lucky enough to find a true Craft "family," but many more are still searching. Coven dynamics can be difficult even in the best groups. Finding a coven that fits your beliefs and lifestyle can be tricky, but it is not impossible.

The average Witch who wishes to be part of a coven will likely be part of several over the course of a lifetime. As personal needs change, as people move away, as more families grow up in the Craft, and as fewer people feel they have to practice this religion in secret, our coven structures will change to accommodate us or they will cease to serve their purpose. Covens will be born, they will flourish, and they will die. In keeping with our belief in the eternal cycles of life, many of the covens—through the efforts of remaining members—will be reborn to serve again. Like all reborn souls, they will draw on their past, but there will be new faces, new rituals, and new experiences to cherish.

I have been part of several covens and networking groups since I began seriously studying Witchcraft more than fifteen years ago. Like many of today's newcomers to the Craft, I first undertook a self-initiation, then promptly set about searching for a coven to join. Through pure, blind luck I managed to connect with a very large coven in the community and, in 1983, was initiated into their circle. At the time I was so thrilled to have found others who, I supposed, thought and felt as I did, that I did not stop to consider if this was the right group for me or not. It did not occur to me that, just because this group called itself "Wiccan" (a name applied to some Anglo-Saxon-Celtic traditions) they might not view the Craft, the cycle of the year, the deities, or anything else in the same way I did. I also did not have the experience at that point to understand that this difference of opinion did not necessarily make me wrong and them right, nor was it a sign that I should rethink my hard-won spiritual values. This was merely a difference in how we chose to outwardly express our faith.

Fortunately, I went into this venture with a close friend, and the two of us were able to eventually sort out that this coven, through no fault of its own, was just not for us. It was full of good, knowledgeable people who just happened to have theological viewpoints to which we could not conform, and preferred a strict hierarchical coven structure in which neither of us die-hard egalitarians felt comfortable.

We wished the coven well, parted ways, and began working together as a coven of two. During the next couple of years our skills grew along with the public's renewed interest in Witchcraft. Networking with others, including solitaries and people who were part of larger groups, became easier, and opportunities for group worship more numerous. We discovered that study groups and networking organizations also had a place in our lives, and that we need not be limited to working with only one group, or expressing our spirituality through only one Craft tradition.

In January of 1986 I met a woman at an Irish dance in Houston who became my mentor and teacher. Through her, I became part of a network of teaching covens that taught Irish and Wiccan Witchcraft. I was part of this family-like group until I moved away from Texas four years later. It was one of the most rewarding experiences of my life.

Why a Book about Covens?

This book was written to serve two purposes. First and foremost, if you are a practicing solitary Witch—one who either by choice or chance is not affiliated with a larger coven or group—I want to have the chance to immerse you vicariously in the world of covens. By glimpsing what they are really like—both the positive and the negative— you will be in a better position to decide if becoming part of a coven is right for you. More importantly, this information will help you decide to which type of group you are best suited. After all, experience is the best teacher, and even if you have been alone in the Craft for a decade or more, and are extremely knowledgeable, being part of a coven is a whole different way of life with unique frustrations and rewards.

Second, for those of you who already know, or who decide while reading this book, that you definitely want to be part of a coven, I hope to be able to provide the tools you need to succeed. The mechanics of connecting with other Witches can sometimes be perplexing, and stumbling along hoping to meet your perfect spiritual mates can be a long and frustrating struggle. I know. I have been there. I've stumbled, fallen, and picked myself up to start again time after time until I finally found what I was seeking. I know it can be done—safely and enjoyably—and that if you are really willing to work at it, you can find or create the coven of your dreams. If you have already stumbled and are tired of skinning your knees, I hope to give you the courage to try again. Trust me, the results are well worth the effort.

For those unfamiliar with Witchcraft who may have picked up this book hoping to read a sensational exposé full of titillating dark secrets we Witches never wanted the world to know, you are to be sadly disappointed—but, please, keep reading! I hope that by the time you have finished this book you will have lost the sense of the sensational that grips you when you hear the words "Witches' coven." Learning that Witches do not worship the devil, do not drink the blood of children, and do not slay animals to appease some perverted notion of deity will help you realize that Witchcraft is simply a religion, one that happens to meet in small, private circles during the changing times of nature rather than in a large building once each week. We are a mystery religion whose inner secrets simply cannot all be put into words, but must be experienced by the seeker.

If this is the first book on Witchcraft you have picked up, be aware that it is not intended as a substitute for a book on basic Craft teachings. Other excellent books admirably fill this need. If you are interested in learning more about the history, beliefs, and practice of Witchcraft, please look in the appendix at the back of this book for the names of some books and authors I highly recommend.

To sum it up, Witchcraft is a branch of Paganism. This is similar to saying that Methodism is a branch of

Protestantism. Within the larger picture of these respective faiths are many variations, though they all share certain similar viewpoints and objectives.

When one defines oneself as Pagan, it means she or he follows an earth or nature religion, one that sees the divine manifest in all creation. The cycles of nature are our holy days, the earth is our temple, its plants and creatures our partners and teachers. We worship a deity that is both male and female, a mother Goddess and father God, who together created all that is, was, or will be. We respect life, cherish the free will of sentient beings, and accept the sacredness of all creation.

Witchcraft is not just an excuse to make magick or shock our elders. Anyone can engage in these acts without going to the trouble of studying the Craft. The study period is a time of work and growth, and no one becomes a Witch overnight. Traditionally it takes a year and a day of study, either alone or with a teacher, before formal initiation or dedication can occur. Those who are not serious usually drop out long before initiation time.

Witchcraft is a *religion,* so the worship of the God and Goddess, and our seeking to know and merge with them, is its central purpose and not an afterthought. The Craft will not proselytize to win converts, but expects the postulant to seek the path to knowledge on his or her own. Like other religions, Witchcraft is based on a system of ethics. We sum these up in our Rede: *As it harms none, do what you will.* This is a first cousin to the Golden Rule of Christianity, and, to borrow a term from a popular science fiction world, it is our *prime directive.*

Witchcraft, or Wicca as it is sometimes called, is a branch of Paganism from western Europe, notably from

Ireland, Britain, and Saxony and, to a lesser extent, from other sections of the northwestern portion of the European continent. The etymology of the word has been argued *ad nauseam* in recent years, with two schools of thought prevailing: 1) That the word derives from the Old English word *wyk*, meaning "to bend or shape," or 2) that it comes from the Anglo-Saxon word *wit*, meaning "to have knowledge or wisdom."

Many centuries ago Witchcraft, called by many different names, was the prevailing religion of Europe. There were no covens at that time. Religious rites were celebrated by entire communities, perhaps led by priests or priestesses who had studied for many years in a special order to be worthy of the honor. Covens as we know them probably developed in the Middle Ages, when the Christian Church began to seek out and destroy the followers of the old Gods, and coming together in secret was the only way the old ways could be preserved, practiced, and taught.

Like other religious organizations, covens today may serve social and cultural functions, but their primary purpose is still spiritual. We join covens to worship, to revel in the presence of the divine, and to seek the ancient mysteries and celebrate creation. Within the diversity of coven structure there is a niche for almost everyone.

Welcome to the world of the Witches' coven, where something magickal awaits those who come seeking. Blessed be all who enter our circles.

Chapter 2

Which WITCH'S
COVEN is Which?

ALL COVENS ARE DIFFERENT in basic character because
the people who are part of them are different in character.
However, covens also share many similarities simply
because they are all part of nature religions, and therefore
built upon the same fundamental tenets of faith. The
greatest differences between them are not so much theological as structural. The greatest diversity occurs in the
following ten categories. They can make all the difference
to someone who is searching for that "perfect" group.

Hierarchical or Priestly Covens

In some covens, leadership and rank are strictly defined
by the "degree" or level of expertise attained by each

Witch. These covens are said to have a hierarchical structure. Degree systems vary from tradition to tradition, and even from coven to coven. It is not unusual to have as few as three or as many as five degrees. To advance in any of these degrees the applicant is required to complete a prescribed program of study, and then be initiated into each one separately by someone of equal or higher rank.

In general, the degree divisions are:

Neophyte: A Craft student still working on his or her first year and a day of study in preparation for basic initiation as Witch.

First Degree: Witches who have been initiated, but have not undertaken any advanced study, either by choice or because not enough time has passed to allow them to take another degree. In some traditions this degree also confers the first level of priest/priestesshood, at which the Witch is considered capable of carrying out his or her own ritual obligations.

Second Degree: Witches who have intermediate knowledge of the Craft and who have usually been involved for at least two years. Many traditions confer priest/priestesshood on this degree.

Third Degree: In many hierarchical covens this is the minimum level that must be achieved in order to be considered a High Priest/Priestess. This person has studied the Craft in depth, is usually a teacher, and may be a leader of not just one, but of many covens.

Elder: Some traditions require an elder to have been active in the Craft for a minimum number of years, as well as to have demonstrated advanced knowledge and provided service to the Craft community. Others only require proof that sufficient knowledge has been obtained by working with another elder.

Just because someone tells you he or she is a "Grand Exalted Orthodox High Elder Priest," anointed by (fill in the name of any well-known Witch here) does not mean that she or he is more qualified than you are to be a leader or teacher, or that this person's opinions should be taken as carved-in-stone law. Unless you know this person very well, you may not even be able to assume that he or she is telling the truth! Unfortunately, some folks just can't resist fabricating their personal Craft history in order to take charge of a group. Since such information is fairly easy to verify in today's closer Craft community, this game is played less often than in the past—but it still happens. Also remember that someone who is an elder in one tradition—though deserving of your respect by virtue of the time spent in training—may not have any status outside of that tradition. Compare this person to a Catholic priest addressing a group of Methodists. The priest would be respected for his learning and achievements, and his opinions would be of interest, but they would not be binding upon the Methodists.

By contrast, priestly covens do not have this degreed structure and are much more egalitarian in their approach to coven work. However, they do not skimp on their expectations for students and newcomers. For example, in my tradition we expect newcomers who have already been initiated as Witches, or who have done a self-dedication, to take up to another full year to learn our particular expression of the Craft. At the end of that time they are encouraged to continue learning to become a priest or priestess, after which they may share in the leadership of the group and help teach others.

Leadership positions within a priestly coven often rotate among qualified members, and group decisions are made on a consensual or rotating basis. Many of the priestly traditions focus heavily on the idea that each individual has a patron deity, and priests/priestesses will often take their vows of initiation by declaring themselves to be priests/priestesses of a specific deity.

Initiatory or Non-Initiatory Covens

Some covens require that one of their leaders initiate you into their group in order for you to be considered a part of that group or its tradition. These are called initiatory covens. Non-initiatory covens will accept your word that you have done a self-initiation after a year and a day of study, or will accept your initiation by another group or another tradition.

In either case, when you join a new coven, be prepared to undergo some type of formal induction into the group, even if it is just taking an oath of loyalty to the other members. (See Chapter 5 for more information on coven initiations.)

Traditional Witchcraft or the Eclectic Coven

In Paganism, a tradition compares to a sect in one of the mainstream religions. For example, all Presbyterians are

Protestants, but not all Protestants are Presbyterians. A sect is merely a division of the larger faith, and has its own ideas about how that faith should be expressed.

Most of the Craft traditions we hear about today were formed within the last forty years, though many of the beliefs and practices found within them are ancient. Traditions usually form around a specific culture and an idea of how that culture's indigenous spirituality was or should be expressed. For instance, the Seax-Wican tradition was founded by Raymond Buckland in 1973, but its practices are based on spiritual beliefs of the old Saxon people that have been made relevant for today's Witches.

Literally hundreds of traditions are flourishing today. Among the better known are the Gardnerian, named for English founder Gerald Gardner; the Alexandrian, named for founder Alexander Saunders, who incorporated lots of ceremonial magick into the Craft; the Maidenhill, another English-based tradition; and the Faery, a hierarchical Irish path popular in the United States.

Witches who follow no single tradition, and who feel free to take from all Pagan cultures as they see fit, are called Eclectic Witches. Logically they call their faith Eclectic Wicca. At the full moon the eclectic Wiccan might invoke the Greek Goddess Selena, at Bealtaine (May 1) she might call upon the Celtic God Cernunnos, and on a new moon she might evoke the presence of Baba Yaga, a Russian crone Goddess.

Because Eclectic Wicca is easily the most popular form of the Craft, it is safe to say that eclectic covens are the most numerous. They are also the easiest to pull together. Witches who might prefer to practice a particular tradition, but who know no one else to practice it with, can feel at home in an eclectic group while still having the chance to work occasionally with their own deities within the eclectic setting. Eclectic covens can also provide you with the basis of a good networking system for meeting others who do share your special interests. There is no rule that says you cannot work separately with anyone you meet while you are still part of the larger eclectic group.

Skyclad or Ritual Dress Options

Another big reason for division between covens has to do with ritual dress. Some covens work in robes, the color and style chosen by the group. Others work in modified street clothing, and a few go skyclad.

"Skyclad" is a fancy term for ritual nudity; it means "to be covered only by the sky above." This concept appears to have been introduced to the Craft in England in the early middle part of the twentieth century. Although it has been argued to be a much older practice, there is little or no evidence to support this claim. Proponents of this practice cite expressions of freedom, equality, and viewing each other as deity incarnate as their primary reasons for choosing this option.

This book does not allow for a detailed discussion of the pros and cons of ritual dress. The important thing to remember is that few covens allow for the mixing of robed and skyclad members. This does not usually work well outside of larger multi-group gatherings, so you must decide long ahead of time what type of dress you will want in any coven you create or join. Also consider why you have made the choice you have. Be honest with yourself, don't allow yourself to be coerced into a choice you will not be happy with later, and do not attempt to coerce others. Remember our Rede! If all you want to do is gawk at naked people, buy a magazine. If you really view your deities as unclothed, and are sure you can best view your fellow coven members as expressions of deity if they are nude, too, then go for it.

The culture in which you grew up, and the location where you received your Craft training, will also have a bearing on your choices of ritual dress. English-speaking North America tends to be a more prudish society than that of our European cousins, and these feelings are carried into our Craft experiences. It has often been said that robed groups are the standard in North America, and skyclad groups the norm in England.

Substance Use or Substance Free

When we refer to substance use in a coven we are most often talking not about illegal drugs, but about alcohol and tobacco used as part of religious ritual. Some covens will modify their practices to accommodate the special needs of those who join their groups; others will not.

Tobacco in ritual is used as an offering, burned as a smudge (a purifying incense), or smoked in a communal pipe that is passed among members. Alcohol, usually wine, is used in similar ways. Both can present problems if someone in the coven has asthma, heart problems, or allergies, or is trying to quit smoking or is in recovery from alcoholism.

A few covens use other drugs to induce altered states of consciousness. If this choice is presented to you, you will

have to make up your own mind and live with the conse-
quences, good or bad. My feeling is that drugs are a
crutch. If you want to be a Witch of any power, then you
should be training your mind to do what you will it to do
without the props.

Teaching or Non-Teaching Covens

Some covens do not like teaching because the members
do not want others intruding on their hard-won family
atmosphere. They certainly have that right. Other covens
will take on newcomers, Craft students who work both
with an individual teacher and with the group as a whole,
to learn the basics of Witchcraft or of the tradition practiced by the coven.

The best coven I was ever a part of was involved in a
network of teaching covens. My belief is that teaching
covens perform a great service to the Pagan community
by providing solid entry points that might otherwise be
closed. By giving newcomers a sound start, rather than
abandoning them to their own devices, we strengthen the
Craft community as a whole, especially when these folks
eventually take on students of their own.

Open Circles or Closed Covens

Like the non-teaching covens just mentioned, closed
covens like to keep to themselves. They are generally not
interested in newcomers, and they rarely open any of their
events to outsiders. This does not not mean that they do
not network with other groups by attending large festivals

together. It just means that they keep a low profile and do not expect others to apply to join to their group.

Open circles are covens that have all or some of their gatherings open to interested outsiders. The definition of an open circle may also include study groups and discussion circles wherein rituals are enacted (see chapter 3). These open circles are great places for newcomers to get a taste of coven practice without committing themselves.

Single Unit or Outer Circle/Inner Circle Covens

Single unit covens are similar to the closed covens just discussed. They are usually not looking to expand at this time, and do not often host open rituals or teach others.

Covens with an inner and an outer circle try for the best of both worlds. The inner circle is the heart of the coven, the family-like group that meets regularly. The outer circle is one overseen by the inner circle, usually composed of newcomers, students, or interested others. At some time in the future, members of the outer circle may be asked to join the inner group, or these outer circle people may move on to other covens, or even form a coven of their own based on their positive association within the outer circle.

Fam Trad Covens or Community Groups

Some covens extend no further than the family unit. In the Craft these are known as "fam trads," a contraction of the words "family traditions." They have their own set of rituals and rules, and often focus on honoring common ancestors and responsibly raising the next generation of Witches. It is likely that no one will ask you to join a fam trad unless you marry into one.

Community groups are what we usually think of when we hear the word "coven." They are made up of non-related people, although there is no rule against two or more family members joining an outside coven together.

Gender Segregated or Mixed Gender Groups

The majority of covens are open to both sexes, and it has become customary—but oh so hard to achieve!—to try to have an even number of male and female members to balance the circle's energies.

There are many covens that are composed of all female members. Sometimes this is simply because no men have asked to join; other times the women just feel more comfortable on their own. Women who have felt demeaned by their birth religions often have trouble worshiping male deities, and many admit to having trouble seeing the men in their circle as images of the divine. Others are feminists who feel that they must balance the male-dominated world of religion with one that is all female.

All-male covens are much rarer, but they do exist. Men segregate themselves for many of the same reasons that women do. Patriarchal religion has given them a model of the divine that is harsh, judgmental, and removed from the reach of the average human male. In these all-male covens, men can reclaim the old Gods as their own,

Gods who are more like they are, and who are accessible to their psyches.

While gender divisions are not uncommon in the Craft, age and racial divisions are. Although such divisions are not unheard of, you should be wary of the motives behind them. In the Craft, persons of all ages and backgrounds are respected for being who and what they are. The only exception to this may be in regard to minors. Persons under eighteen who join covens can lead to legal problems for groups. Some outraged parents are sure that their precious bundles of joy have been spirited away by a mind-perverting cult. If you are under eighteen you will have a much harder time finding a coven to join, or enticing older persons to be part of any coven you form.

Which Coven Is Right for You?

Before you begin searching for a coven, you should learn as much as you can about Witchcraft from other Wiccans/Pagans, books, Pagan periodicals, and any other materials you can find. The more you know, the more easily you will fit into group situations, and the more interested a coven will be in having you as a contributing member. Anything you need to learn about the particular tradition of a coven will be taught to you after you join the group.

Begin deciding what type of coven you should be in by giving yourself a little mental examination. Start by looking at the way you have related to others in group situations in your past. Have you always had the urge to run things? Are you a natural leader? If so, you may need a coven in which you can rise to the top of the hierarchy. Do you tend to be dictatorial or quarrelsome? If so, you may need a strict hierarchy that will keep you on the bottom for a long time, just to teach you lessons in humility and getting along with others. In group situations, are you always the one who tries to patch up arguments and help everyone get along? You might do best in an egalitarian setting, where your talents will be appreciated and used.

Aside from helping you decide what type of coven might be best for you, personal examination can help prepare you mentally for how you will contribute to the group's dynamics. As the old maxim goes, forewarned is forearmed. You can begin to overcome your negative group traits in advance, *before* they have a negative impact on a group.

Your "Must-Haves" List

As you read and talk about the Craft with others, do so critically, always questioning and making notes on the things you like and don't like about different practices or concepts. Especially note anything you come across that appeals to you greatly or repulses you entirely. These are the items on which you will not likely be open to compromise in a coven situation. They are the issues most important to you, and you will need to use this information to help you decide what you are looking for as you begin your quest for a coven.

Be picky as you list these "must haves." If you don't, you will only be unhappy later on, and you will likely make the rest of your coven miserable, too. Being picky means deciding what type of coven structure and spiritual interaction you are seeking, not how you want your fellow covenors to look and think. If you automatically dismiss the young man with the long hair and earrings, the old woman with the ten spoiled cats, or the overweight housewife who peppers her speech with the latest New Age slang, you may be cheating yourself out of a terrific coven experience due to nothing more than prejudice. Instead, focus on inner qualities, and how these will be manifested in a group situation.

When you have completed your list, reread it. Ask yourself if your list contains reasonable expectations. If not, strike them out. Be open to human shortcomings, and be willing to compromise on the issues you feel the least strongly about.

My own standing list of requirements follows. It is not meant to be a guideline for your own list, but is intended to show you that where one Witch has firm ideas about certain areas, other Witches (perhaps yourself) might find these same areas unimportant.

1. Works robed or in modified street clothing.

2. Has an egalitarian/priestly structure.

3. Expects all members to contribute according to their ability, and all are included in planning sessions.

4. Will accept both Witches who have been initiated by other groups and those who have done self-initiations.

5. Strict substance-free atmosphere.

6. Maintains an outer circle or teaches sincere newcomers.

7. Adheres to a written compact (see Chapter 4) that has been ritually sworn to or signed by all members, and that covers all important aspects of coven life.

8. Views sacred space as safe space for all.

9. Allows for flexible meeting times.

Notice that I do not make a requirement of my preferred tradition in my must-haves list. While I would always prefer to be part of a coven that follows my own tradition, this can be difficult to achieve. I am just as comfortable in an eclectic setting where I can share my tradition's knowledge and learn from others as well. We are all free to practice our individual traditions on our own while still being part of a coven that, being eclectic, strives to meet everyone's spiritual needs.

The last item in my list—"allows for flexible meeting times"—is one upon which I always insist. Modern life simply does not permit a half dozen or more people to clear their schedules for every full moon or every solar festival. Nor does it allow for the average person to meet at "traditional" times: midnight for the full moon, sunrise for the Spring Equinox, noon for the Summer Solstice, et cetera. With luck, there is usually one afternoon or evening each week when everyone is free, and these are the times when meetings are best held. I would rather see everyone able to participate on an off date than see people left out because they have to go to work on the official date. I also feel it is preferable to hold rituals at the closest possible date in *advance* of the festival, because the waxing energy of anticipation is stronger than the waning energy of a past event. If you find a group that is flexible enough to meet on the exact dates at the exact times, you are truly blessed! If not, there is no law that says you cannot hold a private ritual at the time when all astrological correspondences are correct. In fact, this is encouraged.

If you share your must-haves list with someone else and they call you a snob, or worse, just ignore them. No one's must-haves list is inherently right or wrong. Remind these people that you have the right to seek the group situation that makes you happy, as do they. Stick to your basic ideals in so far as they are reasonable.

You can magickally charge your list to act as a talisman to attract to you others who share your vision for a coven. To do this, spend some time holding the list in your hands, investing it with your energies and your desire. Then place the list under an orange votive candle that is safely inside a glass candle holder. Orange is a color of attraction and friendship. Light the candle, seeing it as a beacon reaching out across the darkness of space and time, calling others to you who share your desires. You might see it functioning like a magickal lighthouse, illuminating dark waters and making them navigable to your home port. Make sure to allow for the free will of any who might be attracted by your light. Spend as much time as you can watching the candle, meditating on what you want, and continuing to focus energy on your goal.

Chapter 3

NETWORKING and
GROUP DYNAMICS

SOLITARIES AND NEWCOMERS FREQUENTLY ASK, "How
do I meet other Witches, and where do I find a coven?"
My answer is always that you are very unlikely to "find" a
coven that will just pick you up off the street and make
you one of their own, at least not any coven of which you
would really want to be a part. If you really do want to be
part of a coven, you will first have to do some serious networking on the local level, seeking out and getting to
know other Witches as people before you can appreciate
them as Pagans.

Precautions When Meeting with Strangers

Just because the people you are hoping to connect with
ostensibly share your spiritual views, you cannot rely on

this to protect you from unscrupulous or dangerous individuals. Chances are that the vast majority of your contacts will be sincere people who wish you no harm, even though they may not all share your vision of what a coven should be. Sadly, however, we live in a world in which being cautious when dealing with strangers is a necessity. It is better to be overly cautious now than desperately sorry later.

When I first began in the Craft I thought that my precautions were protecting me from outsiders who did not understand what Paganism was all about, such as the fundamentalists who would rather revive the anti-Witchcraft laws than find themselves living next door to one of us. Experience changed my focus and forced me to admit that I keep my guard up against other so-called Witches, not against non-Pagans.

Never give your home address to anyone you do not know well, especially if you live alone. Get a post office box or, if possible, have mail delivered to your office or work address. E-mail is another option that helps protect your personal identity and home address. Through the mail, arrange to meet your contacts at a well-populated, neutral location. I have always been fond of meeting new people for lunch, or for coffee in the evening, at busy restaurants. After your initial meeting, you will have a better idea of how much more information, if any, you wish to exchange.

A woman acquaintance, who belonged to one of the same networking groups in San Antonio as I, had her home burglarized one day while she was at work by someone she trusted too well, too quickly. While this is not the usual result of meeting with other Witches, her experience should nonetheless remind us to exercise prudence.

Be stingy with your phone number as well, unless you have an employer who does not mind your taking personal calls at your work number. Home phone numbers can be changed with relative ease if you do run into problems, but it is best not to court a bad situation in the first place. Though I have always been careful about my address, I used to see the phone as a safe haven, and I was too generous with my phone number. In the fall of 1988 I was harassed with a series of 'round-the-clock phone calls from a contact I had made. Fortunately, the person doing the calling did not know me very well or he would have been aware that I—a confirmed night owl—was wide awake when the calls came in at night, and I always kept the phone turned off during the day so I could sleep in peace. Though my life was basically unaltered by the calls themselves, the messages on my answering machine became increasingly annoying, even a little frightening.

When my lack of verbal reaction to the calls failed to give the caller the kick he was looking for, he set out to learn my home address and, eventually, succeeded. At first, I found nothing more than an assortment of odd "gifts" left for me on my doorstep. Then the caller decided that vandalism of my property would better attract my attention. Being a night person, and having night people coming at all hours to and from my house, cut down on his destructive opportunities, but knowing someone was watching my home so closely was unnerving. I was finally forced to contact the police, after a series of letters arrived containing threatening messages that the guy had been stupid enough to sign.

I have never had to deal with anything like that since, and I know many Witches who have never had to deal with harassment at all. However, you should be aware of the potential for trouble, and exercise caution with common sense. Remember that some people are attracted to Witchcraft for the wrong reasons, usually because they are seeking power or control over others, and they have little interest in spiritual ethics.

Craft names, the "handles" we choose for ourselves when we dedicate ourselves to the Craft, are very useful to help protect identities. Some Witches believe these should be used only inside the ritual circle, and not in public, but a great many Witches today use their Craft names, or some variant form of them, any time they are interacting with other Pagans. You may wish to consider having such an alias as you begin networking. It is a lot harder for someone with negative intent to find the home address of Willow Moonsinger than of Lisa Jane Smith.

Another people problem that is more irritating than unpleasant is the existence of chronic problem folks. All religions have them: the hangers-on whose lives are just never right, who always have a list of woes that their new-found religion and all who embrace it will certainly help them overcome. They take no positive steps forward, and feel no sense of responsibility for any part of their situations. Know this now, before you even get started networking—there are lots of these folks out there, all looking for a magick pill cloaked in a ritual robe. They will demand your attention, take up too many hours of your time, and suck away at your personal energy with all the zeal of a thirsty vampire. In the name of compassion, you may at first feel moved to help them. I know. I have been there too many times, and I have learned you cannot help these people. They do not really want our help. Ten years from now the only thing that will have changed in their lives is the name of their religion and the faces of the people they are whining to for advice they never take. If you run across one of these entities, gently send it on its way with love and blessings—but don't waste your time.

Networking

Whether you want to create a huge web of covens, or just find one or two Pagan/Wiccan friends, you have to start by networking. Networking means reaching out and finding other Witches/Pagans with whom to begin building friendships, and through whom you can meet others. The network you build can be used to form study groups or covens, or just provide mutual support and friends who share the same interests. The choice of what you do after your network is in place is yours alone, but first you have to get out in the community and do the leg work.

Witches don't advertise in the yellow pages. Almost any of us who have ever connected with others had to make the effort to do so. Of course, you will have a few lucky breaks, but for the most part only diligence will lead to success. I often get letters from readers all over North America who want me to tell them where they can find a local coven, and I know other Wiccan/Pagan writers who are deluged with similar requests. The truth is that most of us do not know where all the covens are in our own hometowns, and we know nothing about the Craft community in areas we have never visited. Even on the off chance that we do know of a contact near you, we are usually not at liberty to divulge that information unless we know that group is advertising open circles or actively seeking newcomers. If this is the case, then you can find these folks much easier than we can through local networking.

The best place to start is in the pages of periodicals that are regularly read by Wiccans/Pagans. The names of some of these can be found in the appendix in the back of this book. The contacts, personals, or networking columns of these magazines may point you to local groups or gatherings. If any of the publications are produced in a city near you, you may find that they carry more local news and information than similar periodicals from across the continent.

Local newspapers or journals that serve alternative lifestyles can be useful too. These publications cater to people interested in a wide variety of non-mainstream activities and beliefs, such as vegetarianism, animal rights, gay issues, New Age thinking, and all forms of alternative spirituality.

No matter which periodicals you read, look for announcements of open circles or Pagan festivals taking place near you. An open circle occurs when a coven hosts a community ritual for all who are interested. Through them you may find others who are searching for the same things you are. Pagan festivals are large gatherings that usually take place around the solar holidays (see Chapter 8) and, depending on the size and fame of the festival, can draw hundreds of people from a wide geographic area. Also keep an eye out for advertisements for news of lectures or classes at local bookstores and occult shops that might attract other Witches.

You might want to peruse any biographical information about a magazine's contributors. You never know what you might find. As I write this, I have been back in my home state of Indiana for just over two years. During the first year I was so busy rearranging my hectic lifestyle around all the major changes I had made that I ignored the advice I often give to solitaries not to cut themselves off from the larger community, even if they ultimately prefer to worship alone. A friend of mine who had just become interested in the Craft happened to see a bio note after an article in a local alternative newspaper that was written by a Wiccan woman. Included in the bio was her mailing address. My friend wrote to her and arranged a lunch meeting. She came back enthusiastic and swore that I just had to meet this person, that she knew we would get along great. I agreed to the meeting—thank Goddess!—and now have a wonderful friend and contact in that woman.

Admittedly, not all bio notes will be so blatant in their proclamations that, yes, this writer is a Witch. Sometimes you may have to read between the lines. As you grow in your knowledge of Witchcraft, this will come easier. You will find that you can recognize your co-religionists by words they speak, symbols they wear, or even by the way they conduct themselves. When my husband was employed within the confines of mainstream Judaism, he knew he had to keep his Judeo-Pagan practices (sometimes called "Jewitchery") out of the congregation; on the other hand, as long as he didn't mention the "P" word, he found he could be very open about his interest in Kaballah (Judeo-Christian mysticism), and often found surprising contacts through these exchanges.

Sometimes a simple word uttered in the presence of someone trained to pick up on it will give you a contact. Many years ago I supplemented my writing income by doing freelance advertising copy. Every Monday morning I went to the restaurant of a client to pick up the information I needed for that week's ad. The manager was inevitably late for our meetings, and I usually passed the time talking with a young waiter who came in to set up before opening. Our routine was that I would sit with him and chat while helping him fill the salt shakers. One morning he toppled a full salt cellar onto the floor, and we began joking about superstitions involving spilled salt, and throwing the stuff around while uttering nonsense words. I forget now just how the conversation progressed, but at some point I said something about casting a salt spell, to which he replied, "That's not how you cast a spell." As I got up to catch the manager, who had just walked in, I said, "I know." We verbally danced around each other the following Monday morning, each tossing out little hints and verbal tests until we were each confident that we were talking to another Witch.

Some Pagan networking directories have been published that attempt to link the Craft community, though these are only as thorough as the willingness of people to make public information about their group or coven allows. Look in the appendix for more information on these directories.

If you live in a larger city, you may find that occult shops, natural food stores, or metaphysical and feminist bookstores can provide a point of entry into your own Pagan community. Check out any bulletin boards or newsletters they produce, or ask about classes or meetings that may be held at their locations. Be sure to ask the store owner or manager about open groups or other Witches in the area looking for contacts. I have known of several study circles who have given a contact name to bookstores just in case anyone inquired.

If you live in a city that has a Unitarian Universalist Church (look in the yellow pages under CHURCHES), call the church office and ask if they sponsor a CUUPs (pronounced "cups") organization. CUUPs is an acronym for Covenant of Unitarian Universalist Pagans. The church, whose guiding principle is that all religions are valid, often sponsors Pagan groups. This gives the group a safe pace to meet, and allows them to get tax exempt status as legally recognized churches. I have been part of two CUUPs organizations and, though they had different focuses, each was a good place to begin networking. I have even known of covens that were formed from within these groups.

Other legally recognized Pagan churches may be found in the phone book, but more often they are contacted through the classified ads of Pagan periodicals. The Church of All Worlds (CAW), who publish the popular *Green Egg* quarterly, have open circles (called "nests") in many locations, and always welcome efforts to form new ones. (See the appendix for CAW's address.)

Over the past few years some organizations have sprung up whose sole purpose is helping Wiccans/Pagans meet each other. (Again, see the appendix for addresses.) The only drawback is that unless someone in your area has contacted these organizations and requested to be listed as a contact, you may never know they are there. These organizations are likely to grow in size and scope as we burgeon our way into the twenty-first century, and more people should begin to feel comfortable listing with them.

Wiccans and Pagans have made their presence known on the information superhighway with newsgroups, web sites, chat sites, and bulletin boards that cater to those following nature spiritualities. Unfortunately, things come and go quickly in cyberspace, and the popular web site of today may be space dust tomorrow. Your best bet for locating these is to get on whatever search-and-find directory your Internet server provides and look up key words such as WITCHCRAFT, WICCAN, or PAGAN. Connection with any one of these sites will lead you to countless others. Also be sure to ask around at bookstores, occult shops, or computer stores for the phone numbers of local bulletin boards.

Pagans of all traditions are usually very interested in their ethnic heritages; one of my close friends and I made contacts through Irish and Scottish cultural organizations. This method of contact definitely requires more tact than usual, since you do not want to upset the more conservative-minded members of the organization. Keep your ears, eyes, and psychic senses open when talking with people for clues about their spiritual orientation.

After I was interested in moving on from Eclectic Wicca to explore some type of Celtic path, I met the woman who would become my mentor, teacher, and beloved friend. Mollie and I were introduced at a *ceili* (pronounced KAY-lee, and although it means "visit," it refers to an Irish dance party) in Houston by a mutual acquaintance who sensed we had a lot in common. We hit it off right away and spent the rest of the evening on the fringes of the dance just chatting together. Eventually we began discussing pre-Christian Ireland, which naturally led to the topic of Irish Witchcraft. After about an hour of verbally feeling each other out, we let it be known that we were both Witches.

Mollie was part of a network of teaching covens, some eclectic, but most following a variety of Irish paths. At that time her own coven had done a crash and burn because more than half the members had moved away from the area in the past year, and two others decided they wanted to give all their attention to covens following other traditions.

That night she told me a little bit about her tradition, Witta, including all the things she loved about it and the criticism it got from other Irish traditions. No matter what tradition you follow you will always find someone who is eager to criticize it, so be prepared! She said they wanted to reform the coven if they could find enough interested persons who shared their views. Then she asked if I would be interested in meeting the two other women who were still going to be a part the group. I told her I would be very interested.

By this time I had been in the Craft for six years and I knew the precautions to take, the questions to ask, and was prepared to answer any questions asked of me honestly and fully. Mollie's home was between Houston and San Antonio; a week later, the four of us met at a little restaurant just off Interstate 10. We talked for hours, and soon could tell that our energies would blend beautifully. We shared the same basic vision of what a coven should be, as well as sharing similar spiritual goals. I was so excited to have met Witches with whom I felt at home that I couldn't sleep at all that night, and woke my husband to babble excitedly in his ear about the experience.

Several months later the four of us, along with another man and woman, dedicated ourselves as a coven we dubbed *Clan Eireannach*. The name loosely means "Irish Family," and while it is hardly an original name, it fit what was to shortly become a close, family-like group of twelve.

Starting a Regular Pagan Social Gathering, Networking Group, or Study/Discussion Circle

I occasionally get letters back from readers to whom I have made these networking suggestions who complain, "But there are no Craft resources here. I've looked everywhere and tried everything, and there are no Witches. So what do I do now?"

Chances are very good that there is a Witch living near you at this very moment who is giving out the same hue and cry. Someone has to be the first to step out of the proverbial broom closet. Why not let it be you? Start your own group!

Today, networking groups, often in the form of study or social circles, are springing up all over the place. These afford great opportunities to meet other Witches in your area in what is usually a non-threatening setting. There are usually no rituals or vows of secrecy, people drift in and out, and no one expects the group to develop the closeness of a coven. Almost all of my experiences with networking groups have been positive.

The best way to begin, and the one that will keep most people at ease, is to start with a social gathering. Post an ad in all the previously mentioned resources you can get your hands on. State that there will be a social event or coffee clatch for those interested in nature or earth spiritualities at X time in X place. If you don't want to use your own home for a meeting, you might ask the manager of an occult shop or metaphysical bookstore if she or he has a room in which you could meet. Most would probably welcome the increased traffic in their place of business and will accommodate you, at least until other suitable arrangements can be made. Coffee shops located near universities, or other locations where people of different backgrounds gather to chat informally, might also be appropriate places for your meeting. Ask around.

Make sure that the tone of your ad lets potential members know that this is casual "get to know you" event, not an open ritual. Avoid the words "Witch" and "Pagan" in your ad. These words will only stir up the local fundamentalists. Calling it a nature or earth spirituality meeting will get the message across to those who are interested, without unduly alarming the rest of the community. Start slowly and the fledgling coffee clatch of today could turn into the strong coven of tomorrow.

Some of the best covens I have known were formed from study and/or discussion groups. These loosely formed networking organizations are as much social as they are educational. They are easier to get started and to keep going than formal covens, and are less threatening to folks who are unsure about coven work, but who still wish to meet regularly with other Witches. Notices for study groups are often seen in the classified sections of the larger Pagan periodicals. The alternative publications mentioned earlier in this chapter are also good starting points for placing or finding such ads. Bulletin boards—both the physical ones in occult shops, bookstores, or health food stores, as well as the computer boards—carry notices as well.

Study circles or discussion groups take many forms. These gatherings of Wiccan/Pagan folks meet on a regular basis to discuss Craft issues and to learn from one another. Some of them eventually begin ritual work, and a few grow into working covens. Again, posting notices and putting out the word is usually all it takes to bring the local Witches out of the broom closet.

If You Are Using Your Home as a Meeting Site

It is not quite so important to screen potential group members, or to establish firm rules, when your group is meeting at a neutral location like a bookstore. However, many groups meet at the organizer's home, or the homes of other active members, either because they want a home setting or because no other options are available. If you will be using your home as a meeting place, you will need to screen people carefully, and let everyone know up front what the rules will be for your home and for the group.

Having a first meeting with potential group members away from your home is still the safest way to make initial contact. If you feel this person would be an asset to your group, hand him or her a copy of your group's rules. If he or she is willing to abide by these, you've got yourself a new member.

A good, basic set of rules, similar to those used by networking groups with which I am familiar, might consist of the following main points:

1. Respect for everyone's religious feelings, expressions, and traditions. Constructive criticism is fine, but bashing is not. This should include bashing the mainstream religions as well.

2. Some people are nervous about meeting with Pagan groups of any kind, and a few fear exposure of their beliefs to other family members, employers, et cetera. Each member should be able to see the group as a safe place to be. To this end, everyone should be able to trust the other members to protect their identities from outsiders.

3. All members should be expected to contribute to the group as they can. You may want to set modest dues to cover basic expenses, or ask individuals to bring items like candles or food, or to take over leadership on a rotating basis.

4. Rules about substance use in the group should be decided upon up front. The use of alcohol is usually disruptive, and can chase away persons in recovery. Cigarette smoke can aggravate the allergies of sensitive persons, and some folks simply don't like it and do not want to be around it. Whatever you

decide, it should be in writing, so that potential members know what to expect. Don't worry about discouraging members by saying that certain habits or behaviors will not be welcome. You will gain those who share your feelings, others will go elsewhere with folks who share their feelings, and everyone will end up happy because you were honest in the first place.

5. The presence of children too young to contribute to the discussion may not be desirable. The home you meet in might not be child-proof, and small children could unknowingly disrupt meditation sessions, et cetera. This choice is yours to make, and may depend on what kind of members you hope to attract. If you are a young mother who wants to meet other young Pagan mothers, including children could be a big plus. In any case, your policy should be in writing.

6. Many people under eighteen are interested in the Craft, whether they have their parents' permission or not, and they may want to join you. Be warned that, although this youngster might be a sincere seeker with positive things to share, you could be sued by the parents. Such lawsuits have happened already. Sadly, many people still do not understand what Witchcraft is all about. To them, including their child in your circle seems as threatening as having the child sucked into a brainwashing

cult. If any discussion of the roles of sexuality or nudity in the Craft is forthcoming, you are doubly at risk. Either exclude those under eighteen, or require a notarized letter of permission from all parents or guardians.

7. Often, members will want to bring guests to the circle—people you do not know. It is wise to include a rule stating that your permission must be obtained first so that you can get a feel for the person you are inviting into your home. Usually these guests are not involved in any form of Paganism, but are interested in learning what it is their friend is practicing. While this can be a great learning experience for the friend, the inclusion of someone outside the Craft may upset or inhibit your regular members.

8. Emphasize again that your group meets in a private home, and that group members must show respect for personal property and the neighbors' feelings. Some of the homes in which you meet may have small children, and the parents will naturally have concerns about the impact of their guests' conduct on the youngsters. Rowdy behavior, excessive noise, drunkenness, or showing a blatant disregard for the sensitivities of the home owner and his or her neighbors is not only rude, but unacceptable. The last thing you need is the police at your front door, investigating a neighbor's complaint.

Either you, or the person at whose home the meeting takes place, should always be given the unquestioned authority to ask someone who continually breaks these rules past the point of forgiveness to leave. If others choose to side with the disruptive person, and wish to leave also, then you probably have not lost anything. Those who do not respect the needs of a group, or its individual members, will not be the sort of people who will contribute to the growth of the group over the long term. Continue on without them, and be glad you found out what sort of people they were before you became any more involved.

A study/discussion group is not a coven, so don't expect the same level of commitment you would expect from a coven. Whether you meet monthly, weekly, or bi-weekly you are likely to have a solid, core group that meets with you every time and a lot of interested others who drift in and out. As the group members become more comfortable with each other you might try group meditations or brief rituals, if everyone is interested and can agree upon the format.

Above all, allow for a broad discussion of topics, permitting everyone to voice their opinions without fear of censorship or ridicule. None of us is the ultimate authority on Craft matters, and we all have something to teach and something to learn, no matter how long we have studied our faith.

Group Dynamics and Leadership

Anyone who has ever worked with any kind of group is well aware of their fragile nature. It is likely that, if you stop and think about it, you have known or known of at least one person who has stormed out of a meeting in a self-righteous huff. Because of the intense personal feelings we attach to our religious expressions and beliefs, this unfortunate tendency is exacerbated where spiritual matters are concerned.

The word "dynamic" is defined as motion resulting from force. Groups are ever-changing, always gaining or losing momentum as they expand and contract. In other words, group dynamics mean movement and change that are people-driven. Just how that drive occurs is unique to each group.

The character of the individual members has a lot to do with the group's dynamics, which is why you want to carefully screen potential members. It takes only one complainer who is never happy with any choices made, but who rarely bothers to show up for planning meetings; one person who wants to be in complete control by virtue of whatever criteria he or she has set up for him or herself; one inveterate gossip; or one person attracted to the Craft for the wrong reasons (i.e., self-aggrandizement, need for sexual domination, need to exercise control over others, et cetera), to single-handedly destroy even a large, solid coven.

The dynamics of any Witches' coven or group are primarily defined by its leadership, whether that leadership is static, shared, or rotated. The character and attributes of a leader determine whether the coven moves upward and onward, or crashes in flames like a wingless plane.

Good leadership in any group situation requires leaders who do not presume to take charge simply because they believe they know more than the rest of the members. Good leaders accept leadership as a serious responsibility rather than a right. They are honored that you feel they can capably lead you, and work harder than anyone else to make the group work. They take time to listen to everyone's input, from the oldest to newest member, and never belittle any suggestions or comments. Good leaders do not pretend to know all the answers to every question asked. When someone else in the group is clearly the expert in a particular area, good leaders gladly defer to that person. They never lose their tempers with the group, but seek to resolve conflicts in a constructive manner that leaves all members feeling good about themselves and about the group. Good leaders abide by the rules and standards the group has set for itself, and never believe themselves to be above those rules.

If the group rotates leadership roles, when the leadership is working properly the members will gracefully pass on the scepter to the next in line without grumbling or saying, "This wouldn't have happened if I had been in charge."

When the leadership of a group deteriorates to the point that it cannot be fixed, it is time to move on. I was once a part of a social/networking group that I thought would usefully fill in the time between coven meetings. My best friend, Sheva, who was by now following a Scottish tradition, joined too. The group met weekly in the back room of a metaphysical bookstore. The leader of the group introduced herself to us by her Craft name, Thea, which is the Greek word for "Goddess." We thought at first she was a feminist Wiccan, one who follows a tradition that places an emphasis on all of the women in the group viewing themselves as the Goddess incarnate. Later we decided it was because she saw herself as infallible.

Though most of the group's members were in their late teens and early twenties, Thea was in her mid-forties, and clearly some members of the group looked up to her. However, it quickly became apparent to Sheva and me that Thea was hopelessly immature and completely unsuited to lead a group of vulnerable young people. Over the three weeks Sheva and I were in attendance, about a third of the group left, many of them the best people in terms of their Craft knowledge, maturity, and willingness to work with others.

Sheva and I soon realized that the remaining members had all dated each other briefly at some point, and then moved on to conquer other members of the group. Sexuality is more open in Pagan gatherings than in other religious situations, but I have never seen personal relationships handled more irresponsibly than in Thea's network. Many of the members were hurting desperately over failed relationships that they thought were special and, as Sheva pointed out, the meetings were characterized by wounded young people spontaneously bursting into tears.

To make matters worse, Thea seemed to take a perverse delight in fueling the fires of pain burning so near the surface. On one occasion she asked everyone to play a game that involved passing a lemon from person to person using the chin but no hands. The one who dropped the lemon had to claim a kiss from the person passing it to him or her. Sheva and I quickly bowed out of the circle to watch, and were joined by only one other person from a group of about ten people. We sat and watched the other members jockey for positions near someone whose lemon they were determined to drop.

Of course, this game had nothing to do with spirituality or learning Witchcraft, or even with getting to know other members better. As we expected, the game ended with tears. Shrieking, ugly accusations were hurled around like spells gone wild. While the angry words were still flying, Sheva and I quietly slipped out, vowing to ourselves never to return.

After apparently receiving a barrage of complaints about the event, Thea sent a soulful form letter around to everyone, apologizing and saying that she did not realize what trouble she was creating.

Sheva and I did not go back to the group, and we heard it disbanded shortly afterwards. Some months later we discovered that Thea had been under the care of a psychiatrist who had innocently told her she needed to "explore the high priestess" within herself. I am sure that this was intended as a metaphor, not as a suggestion to go out and be a leader of Witches. Thea had only been involved in the Craft for a few months when she formed this group, and not long after its demise she placed herself in a psychiatric hospital.

Being part of the right group or coven is one of the most rewarding personal and spiritual adventures a Witch can experience. On the other hand, falling into the wrong coven—one that is bad in and of itself, or that is just not right for you—can turn life into a living nightmare, and make those days of being alone seem blissful by comparison. For most of us, the risks are worth the rewards. We will keep seeking, planning, meeting, and praying until we find that special group of people that our souls know and love.

Chapter 4

The SENSIBLE WAY to JOIN or CREATE a COVEN

IF YOU DECIDE TO CREATE A NEW COVEN from the ground up, there are questions you need to ask, both of yourself and of those with whom you may be working in the future. If you are asked to join an already existing coven, you need to be as prepared to screen them as they will be to screen you. In over fifteen years in the Craft I have been on both the receiving and giving end of this scrutiny, and have found that the more thorough the questions and answers are in the beginning, the better the working relationship is in the long run.

Don't let the word "working" confuse you. Witches and Pagans often use this term to refer to worship, ritual, and magickal undertakings performed alone or in groups of two or more. Unlike mainstream religious settings, in which the congregation sits passively while someone else stands before them bearing the ritual burden, in a coven all members are expected to pour their energy, attention, and creativity into the proceedings. This is great fun, as well as exciting when it all purrs along perfectly—but it is also a lot more work than most people realize.

What to Look for When Joining an Existing Coven

Before you contact others with the idea of being part of their coven, it is wise to sit down with a calendar and, taking any one month at random, pencil in all of your routine obligations so that you have a chart of your previous commitments. Include everything that demands your time on a regular basis. Mark off your work or class schedule, your week for carpooling the kids to school, the night you take your dog to obedience training, the Sunday afternoon your dance group meets, the one evening a week you and your partner get to go out and relax together, et cetera. About fifteen percent of what is left—and most of us find there is precious little at this point—is the time you can reasonably except to devote to coven activities.

Covens take up a great deal of time. Put bluntly, if you are part of a coven you are expected to be there for planned gatherings unless you have a life-or-death situation at hand, or can make arrangements in advance for your ritual obligations to be fulfilled by someone else. In many covens, everyone is expected to help in planning the rites and bringing certain needed items, as well as carrying part of the ritual load. Those who are habitually unreliable or irresponsible don't last long in most covens. Think about it. If you decide at the last minute that you can't make it to a gathering where you were expected to fulfill certain functions, you leave a large hole in the fabric of the ritual. Not only do you miss the ritual yourself, but you spoil it for others by undermining its maximum effect. Repeated tardiness or absenteeism will probably not be tolerated for long, even if you can manage to make arrangements in advance to be gone. Be very sure you have the time for a coven before you start.

There is no shame in putting off commitment to a coven until your schedule is more open—after your kids are school-age, you graduate from college, you are no longer responsible for the care of your elderly parents, you are not working two jobs, et cetera. If you are bogged down with longterm duties like this, you do not have to resign yourself to loneliness just when you need spiritual support the most. Now is the time to consider networking for friendships, or to find or start a study/discussion group (see Chapter 3).

As mentioned in the previous chapter, you should also honestly list your needs and expectations (your "must haves") before you begin reaching out to the community. If you really can't handle a skyclad group, just say so. Don't agree to join a skyclad coven, then complain later about their practices. If you want a strong leader and a well-defined hierarchy, don't join an egalitarian group that expects you to assume your share of leadership responsibilities. There is no shame in holding out for the coven that best suits you, but there is much shame in knowingly joining the wrong coven, then making everyone else miserable.

After you have made contact with a coven, you may expect to be invited to an informal gathering with the coven members so that they may all get to know you as both a person and a Witch. They will want to see if your ideals are similar to theirs and discover what you can contribute to their group. They will also need to make sure that their energies and yours blend easily. If all goes well at this stage, you will probably be asked to attend a formal ritual, perhaps a monthly gathering at either the new or full moon. Finally, if both you and the group are happy with the results of your participation, you will likely be asked to join the coven.

At some time during this process, it is likely that you will be subjected to an in-depth interview. You might be asked to answer questions about your feelings on the Craft and coven work, and perhaps even to demonstrate your level of skill and knowledge. By asking these questions, the coven members are not implying that they doubt you in any way, so please do not feel insulted or demeaned. This is merely their way of protecting the coven's integrity from those who may not share its focus or viewpoints, or who are not up to speed in their Craft skills (though this is less important if you are going to be a student in the coven). There are many things to be considered when looking at a potential new coven member. Although you may be a knowledgeable Witch and a good person, you may still not be right for this particular coven, and it is best for everyone to find out now rather than later. For instance, if you have been taught that, for certain rituals, a circle should be cast counter-clockwise (banishing rituals sometimes utilize this practice), and the coven firmly feels that this should never be done, you have some decisions to make about how far you are willing to modify your practices and beliefs in order to join this group.

The interview process should not be a one-sided event. A wise Witch will have his or her own set of questions at the ready. If you are involved with the right coven, its leaders and members will not hesitate to answer your questions and address your concerns. In fact, they should welcome them. Your foresight and preparation will demonstrate to them that you are a responsible person who is looking out for all concerned—a big plus in any group situation.

The following is a list of basic questions you might want to ask the coven leaders. Feel free to include others when a situation demands more in-depth scrutiny. There are no right or wrong answers, just ones that feel right to you. Be sure to listen not just to the words of the answers, but note the attitude in which they are imparted and the type of language in which they are couched. For example, I recently ran across someone on the Internet who was looking for "dominions" for his coven, definitely language that starts my inner bells clanging a warning.

- How long has the coven been in existence?
- How many members are in the coven? In general, how many years of Craft experience do they have?
- Are members of both genders? All sexual orientations? Diverse ethnic backgrounds? What is the average age of the members?
- How are new members usually selected?

- How large do you expect to grow? Do you provide for hiving off (splitting into more than one coven) when the group reaches a certain size? (Thirteen is a traditional number for members, but this is hard to achieve and maintain. The number has been said to represent the number of lunar months in a solar year.)

- What is the coven's traditional focus, if any? If eclectic, what leanings do you have (i.e. Celtic, Dianic, Northern, et cetera)?

- Is there an outer circle? Do you teach others? Do you ever host open circles?

- Does the group adhere to the Wiccan/Pagan Rede?

- Is there a coven compact you can read? (See later in this chapter for more about the importance of compacts.)

- What is the coven's internal structure?

- What is the ritual dress? Does it vary on occasion?

- Who prepares the rituals? Are they memorized or read out loud in the circle?

- Who decides how, when, and for whom magick is enacted?

- How often does the coven meet? What happens if you must miss a meeting?

- Aside from these times, what other coven meetings will you be expected to attend? What level of participation is expected?

- Where does the coven meet? Will you be expected to provide a meeting place occasionally?

- Who are the coven's leaders? How did they get these positions? How long will they hold them?
- What other coven officers might there be? How are they chosen? What are their duties? How long are their terms of office?
- Does the coven ever network with other covens or groups?
- What, if any, ties to national or international Pagan/Wiccan organizations are maintained by the coven?
- Are dues charged by the coven? If so, how much? What sort of things are covered by this money?
- If you join this coven, what will be your place in the group, and what is the program for advancement?
- Are identities of members kept confidential? Does the coven have a special policy on the use of Craft names?
- Does the coven maintain a high profile in the local Pagan community? The national Pagan community? In the secular community?
- Is anyone in the coven a licensed/ordained member of the clergy? Is anyone in the group well known in the Pagan community? In the secular community?
- How are inner group conflicts dealt with and resolved?
- How many people have left the coven since its inception? Why did they leave? May you speak

with any of them, with their permission, of course?

- Has the coven ever had to banish a member (see Chapter 11)? For what offense? Without divulging any coven secrets, how was the banishment handled?

- Are there any prohibitions against your being a part of other covens or networking groups while you are a member of this coven?

- Are there vows of secrecy to be taken?

- If you have been initiated before, or have done a self-initiation, is this acceptable to them? Do you have to be reinitiated as a Witch, or just initiated into the specific tradition that is followed by the coven? All of the above? None of the above?

- Without expecting anyone to divulge coven or tradition secrets, what can you expect from an initiation rite? A rite of passage? A magickal working?

- What is the policy on minors at rituals? What are the procedures for inviting guests?

- Are alcohol, tobacco, or drugs used in rituals? How? How often? How would they feel if you abstained?

- What is the coven's view on sexual imagery in rituals? How do they handle personal relationships among members?

- How do they view the circle space? As safe space, or a place where some have power over others?

- Do any rituals involve bondage, fear tactics, or belittling of members?

If you do join an existing coven, it is a wise idea to look over the answers you got to these questions in another few months to make sure that the group is living up to the assurances it gave to you. You might ask yourself the following questions. There are no right or wrong answers, but an honest examination should tell you pretty quickly whether or not you should remain in this coven.

- Does the group seem to have a solid future, or are they wandering aimlessly in some pseudo-spiritual wilderness?
- Is the group meeting my spiritual needs? Am I going to be able to grow spiritually in this group, or will I be better off as a solitary?
- Do I feel a part of the coven on the deepest level?
- Do I like the rituals? How much input have I had in their creation? Have all of the ritual words, symbols, and gestures been explained to me, or am I always left to wonder?
- Do I like the members of the coven as people? Do I like them as Witches?
- Do they seem too anxious to please me or to keep me a part of the group? Do they seem indifferent to my presence and contributions?
- Are the leaders too dictatorial? Do coven members seem to fear the leaders?
- Am I afraid of anyone in the group? Can I build an environment of love and trust with these people?

- Is the atmosphere coercive at any time? Have I been asked or cajoled into doing things I do not want to do? What happens when I refuse? If I have not refused, what has held me back?
- Have I been asked to witness events and situations that I think are wrong, dangerous, or against the Rede?
- What would I change about the coven if I could? What would I not change?
- Have there been any magickal practices or rituals with which I was uncomfortable? Did anyone note my discomfort? If so, did anyone try to put me at ease?
- Am I permitted to speak my mind about making positive changes?
- What happens when I ask questions? Do I get honest and direct answers? Do the more experienced people help me out, or do they belittle my search for knowledge? Do they answer in non-answers, as if maybe they really don't know but want to pretend that they do?
- Do the members get along with one another? Is there a high degree of useless gossip and backstabbing?
- Am I frequently asked to utter words, the meaning of which has not been explained to me?

This last issue is another that sets off my inner warning bells. Being asked to speak words that have no meaning for you is not a spiritual exercise. Ritual is intended to help you forge a link with the divine by connecting your subconscious to your conscious mind. Words you do not know are simply "white noise" in your head; they cannot help forge that link. I have heard of unscrupulous ritual leaders who deliberately plant unexplained words into rituals to gain control over their groups by setting themselves up as the keeper of the great verbal secrets. Sometimes the words are simply made up and have no meaning in any language. These can serve a purpose only if the reasoning is explained to you beforehand. At other times the words are negative words of power, intended to produce harmful magick with which the leader knows you would not go along if you knew the truth. Always question such words in a ritual and, if possible, check them out in a lexicon before speaking them.

Creating a Coven from Scratch

If there are no local covens for you to join, or if the ones you have come across do not share your vision, then you may wish to consider starting a new one. First, take out your list of must haves (from Chapter 2) and begin thinking about the type of coven you want to build. This can be an exciting time, and you should enjoy creating your fantasy coven in your mind. This visualization is magick at its most basic, and fine-tuning your mental image of the coven you want will help it manifest.

After you have a firm idea of the type of coven you want, the next step is to make your intent public with advertisements. Look back at the "Networking" section in the previous chapter to help you locate journals and businesses in which to launch your ad campaign. Remember that you will need to be selective to reach the broadest Wiccan/Pagan audience at the least expense. Stick to magazines Witches are likely to read, and businesses they could be expected to frequent. Don't bother posting notices in the grocery store or sending them to the general press. The only response you are likely to get from these will be from kooks or religious fanatics who will call to tell you that you're going to hell.

The way you word your invitation is crucial. Certain key words can turn off good potential members, or attract the sort of people you do not want. Whatever you do, resist the urge to place an ad that sounds like this:

> *I am starting up my own coven and looking for members. Please write to me. If you sound like what I'm looking for, I will call you. Send photo if possible. Write me at....*

Don't laugh! I have actually seen ads very similar to this one. While we have to admire the writer for going after what she or he wants, overuse of the words "me" and "my" in any coven ad is an instant turn-off. It implies a dictatorial personality, one many Witches can do without. It also conveys the attitude that everything is irrevocably in place except the warm bodies. People don't want to feel that they have no say in a coven's operation, or that they are only cogs in the machinery that could be easily replaced. The line "if you sound like what I'm looking for," without offering any hint of the type of coven or tradition, is much too vague. Subconsciously we wonder what secrets are hiding in between the lines, or whether the person who placed the ad has thought far enough ahead to have secrets.

The best ads approach the idea of a coven as a maybe rather than a given. For the best results try something like the following, which is less threatening than the first example:

Solitary Wiccan with _____ years experience now ready to network with others for friendship and possible coven formation. My focus is eclectic with Celtic leanings. Write to P.O. Box _____ and let me know how to contact you. We can "do lunch" and see how our energies flow.

If you already have a few friends who will be part of the coven, your ad can be made even more appealing. Lots of newcomers want to know there is a real coven already up and running, though they wisely shy away from the "my own coven" ads. One other hint that can help boost your ad's appeal: Eclectic Wiccan groups have the broadest base of interest because they include parts of all traditions. The majority of Wiccans/Pagans are comfortable in them, and rituals within these groups are flexible enough to allow all members to express themselves. Such an ad might look like this:

Small, eclectic, Wiccan/Pagan group seeking new contacts for friendship and possible inclusion in proposed coven or study group. All who abide by the Rede are welcome to write....

When the time comes to screen potential coven members, your best bet is to allow yourself to get to know the applicants over the course of several weeks. Meet often at neutral locations for lunch or coffee; then, when you feel at ease, invite the potential member to your home to meet with the entire group. You may even want the applicant to go through a basic ritual with the coven so that everyone can get an idea of how their energies blend.

When you sit down with the applicant and seriously talk about his or her expectations, allow the applicant to do most of the talking. Letting others do the talking during the screening process will help you get to know the real person and his/her true intent. Train yourself to be silent. People naturally abhor periods of quiet when they are with someone they do not know well, and they will inevitably struggle to fill the void with chatter. This technique can help you screen out the newcomer who is overly anxious to find and belong to a coven, and who will agree to anything just as long as you accept him/her into your fold.

The following is a list of general questions you should consider asking the applicant—but allow the needs of your group or tradition to edit this list as needed. As before, there are no right or wrong answers, only those that feel right to you:

- How long have you been interested in Witchcraft? What led you to this path?
- Do you have a preferred Craft tradition?
- How do you define your religion/spirituality?
- How much do you know of basic Witchcraft? (Allow the applicant to talk at length about circle casting, the elementals, tools, et cetera.)
- Have you been initiated into Wicca/Paganism? By a teacher? By a coven? Self-dedication?

- Have you been initiated into a specific tradition? To what level?
- Have you been part of other covens? Study groups? Why did you leave? How do you feel about these groups in retrospect?
- What do you consider your strong points, both personally and as a Witch? At what magickal skills do you excel?
- What do you consider your weak points, both personally and as a Witch? What skills do you wish to perfect or learn?
- What conflicts, work schedules, or other personal commitments do you have that could interfere with coven meetings?
- How does your family feel about your involvement in Witchcraft?
- What other religions have you followed in the past?
- Are you involved in any ethnic cultural activities related to your chosen tradition? Do you do folk dancing, speak another language, have knowledge of folk crafts, et cetera?
- Are you "out of the broom closet?" (Pagan slang for those who do not hide their religion from the general public.)
- Have you ever taught the Craft to another person? Assess the experience. Is that person still involved in Paganism?
- Why are you interested in this coven and/or this tradition?

- In a best-case scenario, how to you envision a coven? (Allow the applicant to discuss ritual dress, coven structure, leadership roles, and anything else that will give you a clear picture of how he or she envisions a coven situation.)
- What can you contribute to this group?
- What do you expect the group to give to you?
- Do you smoke, drink, or use illegal drugs?
- Are you allergic to incense or wine?
- Do you have any illnesses or physical conditions that could be aggravated by coven practices such as fasting, vigorous dancing, drinking wine, lighting candles, et cetera?

Keep in mind that even if someone's spiritual or magickal energy is not compatible with that of your coven, you do not have to lose this person as a friend or networking contact. Chances are that if you do not feel an applicant is right for your group, she or he will feel the same way, and every effort should be made to part on friendly terms.

If you are part of a teaching coven you will obviously be looking for experienced Witches, unless of course you are screening members for your outer circle. Having come from this type of background myself, I can tell you that the interview process will go more smoothly if you keep a running list of the strengths and weaknesses of everyone in the coven. One simple way to keep up the list is to pass around the coven's Book of Shadows each month and allow members to update their own information as they see fit. This way you will know what you are capable of providing, and what gaps you hope to fill. For instance, if you find a student with a gift for scrying (gazing into objects or elements to induce prophetic visions), you will not want to team that person with a teacher who is weak in this area. We found that, as long as our energies remained positive, we tended to keep our gaps filled and keep our students with the teachers who could do the best for them.

When considering your magickal strengths, list those skills in which you have a high level of proficiency, those that you feel you could teach to others and that don't often fail you. In magick, there is no such thing as 100 percent, no matter how good you are at any skill or how long you've been practicing. Likewise, those items you list as your weak points are not necessarily skills in which you never have any success, just those with which you are not as comfortable and that you would probably not feel secure teaching in depth to others. My own strengths lie in astral projection, dream control and lucid dreaming, herbalism, tarot, and automatic writing. I don't get the results I want every time, but I can count on a very high rate of success, and I rarely hesitate to teach these skills to others when asked to do so. On the other hand, you will likely never see me pen a book on crystal scrying, working with plant totems, or the healing arts. Those are my magickal weaknesses, and I freely admit them.

When all of the interviewing is finished, sit down with the other members of the coven and go over the answers you received (hopefully someone took some notes). Survey them as critically and dispassionately as possible. Try to forget that you and the applicant seemed to hit it off immediately. In most cases your first impressions will be sound—we Witches are pretty good at assessing people—but you don't want to bet your fledgling coven's life on hunches alone. Try to get a feel for the true essence of each answer you received to your queries. Don't lose sight of the issue. You are attempting to determine if the person you interviewed will be a valuable addition to your coven, or a drain on your collective energy. Perhaps meditating or doing a divination will help to further clarify the issue.

The Coven Compact

A coven compact is a constitution by which all members of the group agree to abide. The purpose of this document is to have a structure in place to deal with problems *before* they arise. Think of it as a pre-marital agreement for your coven. When everyone signs, or verbally agrees to the compact in a dedication or initiation ceremony, they each know their responsibilities. No one can come back later and say that they did not know how they were supposed to contribute, how they were to invite others into the circle, how personal conflicts were to be handled, et cetera.

There is no reason to make the language of your compact flowery, and you don't need to write it in fancy calligraphy. Legible writing or typing will do just fine. One copy should be in your coven's Book of Shadows for reference, and another should be given to each member of the group as they join. Open the document with a simple statement of purpose, as shown in the following example:

In order to foster mutual understanding and promote the smooth running of our collective spiritual endeavors, we who are members of the coven now known as

Clan Eireannach do, on this date, September 3, 1986,
create this compact. We consent to work and worship
according to these rules on which we are in full agree-
ment until such time as they are unanimously changed.
Because we cherish what we are building together, we
further agree to swear our sacred oath to uphold this
compact. This oath is no less dear to us than the vows
we make to our Goddess and God of whom we are each
a reflection....

The main points that should be covered in your compact include:

1. A reaffirmation of the coven's commitment
   to the Wiccan/Pagan Rede.

2. A list of basic operating rules, such as those
   that were discussed in the previous chapter
   when talking about study circles. These rules
   will likely be more lax in a coven situation in
   which people get to know one another on a
   more intimate level.

3. It is traditional that learning and practicing
   Witchcraft is a privilege for which people
   should not have to pay, but certain monies
   will be needed for a coven's operating
   expenses (i.e.; to purchase candles, rent a
   meeting site, et cetera). You should state how
   dues, if any, will be collected and how much
   they will be. You may also want to include a
   procedure for amending the dues, or how to
   handle the situation if someone is financially

unable to pay. Sliding-scale fees can work in this instance.

4. If you will be part of a specific Wiccan/Pagan tradition, you may want to state this up front, perhaps listing special attributes of your tradition.

5. Make a general statement about how often the coven will meet—on sabbats, full moons, the first Tuesday of every month for planning sessions, et cetera. State which members are expected to be present (all, officers, teachers, et cetera), and what they should do if they are unable to attend.

6. Make a statement of your expected ritual dress in various situations. For example, robes might be preferred indoors and modified street clothing outdoors. You may also want to discuss any jewelry that will be worn. In some covens, all members wear similar necklaces, or have rings that contain a symbol chosen to represent the group.

7. Make a statement about where the coven will meet, or how meeting places will be decided upon or rotated between members. Remember to be fair. Not everyone has a home or land suitable for coven meetings. Allow these members to contribute in other ways.

8. Decide and outline how to divide responsibility for ritual items and ritual participation.

9. Decide upon and outline your internal coven structure. Will it be egalitarian or degreed,

teaching or non-teaching, open rituals or closed circle? How will leadership be chosen and changed?

10. Outline the duties of each leader so that no one can later point a finger and accuse someone of not doing his or her job.

11. List any other officers your coven will have, and how they will be chosen and changed. Some covens have scribes, keepers of the group tools, coordinators to set up meeting times, et cetera.

12. Clearly outline the duties of these other officers.

13. If you are part of a hierarchical tradition, the compact should discuss how members will move up from degree to degree, and who will be responsible for assessing and initiating them.

14. If you are part of well-organized tradition that has leadership on a national or international level, the compact should discuss your proposed relationship to this body.

15. If you are part of a teaching coven, the compact should outline the duties of teachers and discuss how students will be advanced. Also decide which coven rituals students will be permitted to attend, and what skill or knowledge level they must acquire before attending.

16. If your coven has an inner and outer circle, the compact should address how these will be organized, whether transfers of membership

will occur between them, and if so, how such transfers will be arranged.

17. Make some arrangement for how and when you will handle magickal requests. Certainly the magickal needs of members and their immediate families should be welcome at gatherings during which you deem magickal efforts appropriate, but once others know you are part of a coven, magickal requests will come pouring in faster than you can take them. These usually come from those sorts of people who always have a long list of problems they can't solve on their own, and they will eventually drain every vaporous trace of your spare energy. I have also found that these people are ethical cheats. They would never want to do magick themselves—just in case it really is evil after all, and they wind up in hell for their efforts—but they sure don't mind you taking this risk for them over and over again. Set the limits now. This way when you are faced with a request you do not have the time or energy to handle, you can truthfully state that the governing rules of your coven will not permit the group to take magickal requests at this time.

18. Detail how other members will come into the coven. Some covens want newcomers to seek them out, others will post notices of spaces to be filled when the group feels it is ready to

grow, and still others expect newcomers to be sponsored by a current member.

19. Decide if you will accept other initiations or self-initiations from potential new members, and state this up front. Also note if you have an initiatory tradition that requires initiation into the specific tradition.

20. Briefly discuss how minors or guests may attend a circle. Note that this rule may be subject to change as your group changes in size and scope.

21. Decide how coven decisions will be made—by a majority vote, by consensus, by leadership decree, by rotation, et cetera. Also be sure to include a plan for amending this compact should the need arise.

22. Make some statement about the ritual use of "substances" and stick to it. Also note how these can be made flexible to keep everyone comfortable. You may want to include an affirmation of the sacred space of your circle as a safe space wherein all can feel comfortable, safe, and productive.

23. Decide what will constitute the need for banishment from the circle and how it will be handled. By tradition and by the dictates of common sense, this should be a severe transgression, or even a series of them, that threatens the health and/or lives of members, or that threatens to destroy the group itself.

24. Decide how conflict between group members will be resolved (see Chapter 11 for ideas). By its very nature, a ritual circle magnifies any energy we bring into it. Don't wait until problems arise to decide how to handle them. They won't go away by themselves and, with the circle augmenting them, hesitation will only leave you with one big magickal mess.

25. Include a copy of any group dedication you use at your coven's first ritual (see later in this chapter). This often states the purpose and dreams of the coven in concrete terms.

Two other points are sometimes mentioned in coven compacts. One has to do with expectations about personal relationships between members. We all know that the negative energy from romantic partnerships gone sour can wreak havoc in a group situation, and for this reason some covens ask that members try to refrain from pairing off. While I understand the concern, I have never felt this was fair, particularly since many covens already have legally wed husbands and wives who have been members from the beginning. Another prohibition sometimes mentioned in compacts deal with gossip, though to me this a moot point. If all your group can do is hurl verbal nasties at each other, then you haven't got much going for you anyway.

Because covens change over time, even if you still have all the same faces present, you should take out the compact once a year and look it over as a group just to make sure it is still a viable document that protects the integrity of the coven you have worked so hard to build.

Naming Your Coven

Choosing a name for your coven is another group effort that will likely come early in your association. If you intend to have a formal dedication, the name should be picked well ahead of time. Some covens do not pick a name until they have been together for quite a while, others change their names several times when better names present themselves. There is no right or wrong way to name your coven.

There are many places to gather inspiration when searching for that perfect name. Many covens take their names from magickal objects, heavenly bodies, or things found in nature. Examples of these names are Coven of the Mystic Moon, Coven of the Midnight Tide, Mossy Stone Coven, or The Silver Athame Coven. Others prefer to take a name that provides a cultural designation such as Clan Eireannach, or B'nai Tiferet, the name of a Hebrew-Pagan coven to which my husband once belonged. Still others might honor a patron deity. One all-female group in which I participated called itself Brid's Brood in honor of the Goddess Brighid.

Dedication Rituals for New Covens

We humans like our little ceremonies to mark our achievements, and many covens want a celebratory ritual to commemorate their beginnings. For a newly formed coven, a dedication ritual can fulfill this role, and it will likely be your first group effort at ritual construction.

A dedication serves no major magickal function. It is merely a ceremony to introduce your group to the deities, to pledge your support to each other and to your compact, and to launch your group formally. There are no set rules for doing this rite, and not every new coven does one.

Ideas to commemorate the event include placing small personal items, one from each member, into a time capsule and burying it near your circle site; having all charter members sign the coven's copy of the compact; or having everyone write some of their feelings and thoughts in the coven's Book of Shadows.

When we formed Clan Eireannach we placed a fairly sizeable heel stone at the west end of our circle site—the direction to which our tradition orients its altar—and painted on it the date and our coven's name. Then each of us painted our Craft names on the stone as well, leaving room at the bottom for the names of those who we hoped would be joining our circle later on. The rock served as a symbol of our unity with each other, and with the Earth Mother. Not long after I left Texas, the woman on whose property we met died of breast cancer and her property went up for sale. One of the original coven members could not bear to see the property sold with our heel stone still visible, so one night she snuck out to the circle site with a can of black paint and covered over our stone. I thought this was a fitting symbol of mourning, both for the woman who had thrown so much of her energy into the coven, and for the defunct coven itself.

If your coven will be meeting at rotating locations, large stones are not practical, but coven banners are. These felt, heraldic-style flags that symbolize the coven are easily crafted from felt, glue, and a dowel rod. If you have attended any of the large Pagan festivals, you have no doubt noted these banners whenever entire groups come to the festival together. If you can decide upon a name and symbol for your coven, you can have a banner ready for your dedication ritual. They are always easy to transport from ritual site to ritual site.

Chapter 5

INITIATION
RITES

NOW THAT YOU HAVE FOUND OR CREATED your coven, your next issue will be initiation rites. Initiation is the means by which an individual formally comes into the Craft, or into a particular coven or tradition. In your coven, you may be initiating newcomers into the Craft for the first time or experienced Witches into your coven or tradition, or newcomers into both your coven and tradition. These rites create a line of demarcation, setting the initiate apart from the life she or he had before.

Traditional Elements of a Coven Initiation

Horror movies and bad novels have given the public the idea that there is one great secret initiation rite used throughout Witchcraft, one that is scary and dangerous, involves lots of blood and unpleasant animal organs, and has been carefully guarded and handed down for centuries. Some elements of Craft initiations are probably ancient in theme if not in actual practice, but there is not, and never was, one set formula for initiation rites.

Just as a map shows us a hundred routes to each destination, within the initiation framework there are literally hundreds—maybe even thousands—of possible pathways to initiation. No single path is right or wrong, better or worse. You must choose what suits your personal taste or that of your tradition, then embrace it with joy. Each tradition has its own recommended format, and each coven, whether traditional or eclectic, puts its own spin on things. Because we are all part of one spiritual family, there are some common initiation themes that echo throughout the Craft, but these elements are open to both individual and group interpretation.

The initiation format usually involves many or all of these steps:

- Final testing of the candidate.
- Withdrawal and purification of initiate prior to the actual initiation rite.
- Presentation of the initiate to the coven.
- The ordeal.
- Dedication to the coven and/or tradition.
- Vows or oaths of loyalty and secrecy.
- Adoption of Craft name(s).
- Dedication to the deities.
- Symbolic rebirth.

- Presentation of token of acceptance such as a piece of jewelry or a magickal item.
- Acceptance as full, participating member by coven and/or tradition.

The final testing usually takes place before the date on which the initiation is scheduled, though some covens may incorporate this phase into a lengthy initiation ritual. At this time coven leaders or the student's teachers will administer the last tests to make sure that the initiate knows all she or he needs to know to function as a productive member of the coven. For newcomers this period of study will likely have taken the traditional year and a day. For experienced Witches who are seeking to join a particular tradition, the learning period may be significantly shorter.

Before the initiation, the initiate is expected to arrange for some time alone when he or she can look inward to mentally and physically prepare for the rite to come. This period may be as short or as long as the initiate is able to arrange. As the time for the ritual nears, the initiate will undergo some type of physical purification. This may be done alone, by taking a ritual bath or by following some other prescribed method, or it may be administered by the coven's leaders in the form of a sweat lodge ceremony or some other ritualized purification. In one Middle Eastern coven at which I was a guest, the purification was done within the ritual itself, using olive oil to anoint the initiate as was done in ancient Israel.

At the appointed time in the initiation ritual, the initiate will be presented to the circle to begin the formal rite. It is traditional at this point that an ordeal of some type be undertaken by the initiate, one that tests strength, endurance, or mental prowess. Unfortunately, this has sometimes been interpreted as a need to invoke fear on the initiate. This is called "ordeal by terror."

I have taken exception to these ordeals of terror as a breech of the traditional injunction to covens to meet together in "perfect love and perfect trust." You cannot love and trust what you fear; it is impossible. I find this a sad way to introduce a newcomer to Witchcraft. Some ordeals by terror involve blindfolding, bondage, and even physical torment bordering on the sadistic. Just choosing the Pagan path in a world that still does not fully understand or accept us is fearful enough, especially if the initiate has had to defy the wishes of family or friends in order to join the coven. After making such a commitment, trussing someone up like a Thanksgiving turkey while threatening to skewer him seems pointless.

However, just because blindfolding or bondage is used in the initiation ritual of a coven you are joining, don't assume that an ordeal by terror will follow. Ordeal by terror may occur even if the arms and legs of the initiate are left free, and terror does not necessarily occur when they are bound. Some Gardnerian covens (a tradition named for its founder, Gerald Gardner) have publicized their initiation rites, which involve presenting the initiate skyclad, blindfolded, and with hands tied behind the back. Although this looks miserable, I have never heard a single tale about anyone leaving a Gardnerian initiation ritual harmed or upset. If you have any doubts about whether your coven requires an ordeal by terror, ask now!

More common than ordeal by terror is ordeal by pain. This grew out of an old concept that one must suffer in order to grow spiritually. The method of inflicting pain in modern covens is usually only mildly uncomfortable rather than painful, and often makes use of an instrument known as the scourge, a small whip similar to the sailor's cat-o'-nine-tails. It is beaten about the body of an initiate to purify him or her just prior to the final vows and oaths. I am no more fond of ordeals by pain than by terror, and have never seen that these serve any positive purpose. They also remind me of members of the early Christian Church who routinely inflicted pain and discomfort upon themselves in order to grow spiritually. Obviously, their efforts failed, unless torturing and burning human beings to bring about forced conversions can be considered acts of enlightened spirituality.

I remember hearing one ugly story that made its way through the south Texas Pagan community, about an ordeal by pain that got out of hand. It involved a young woman who began to have second thoughts when the scourge was applied. She declared she was not ready for initiation and asked to be let out of the circle, as should have been her right. The person applying the scourge apparently responded with more force, in an effort to force her to submit. Naturally, being bound and blindfolded as well, she panicked and tried to flee. She was captured, led back into the circle by the rope around her neck, humiliated, and made to continue with the initiation. I have always hoped that this story was not true, and was just one of those tales that gets repeated often enough that it seems true.

Thankfully, most initiation ordeals are not terrorizing or painful, but are symbolic in nature, and involve answering metaphysical questions, or proving that a certain set of tasks can been completed to the satisfaction of the group. I have seen magickal scavenger hunts used in this capacity to great effect, as they test the resourcefulness of the initiate.

After the ordeal, the initiate is presented to the deities and makes his/her vows of loyalty to them. Then, if the coven or tradition has any special secret rites or mysteries that will be revealed to the initiate, she or he must make a vow to hold these sacred. These secrets may be imparted during the initiation or shortly afterwards.

Because virtually all religious traditions view their converts as having been reborn at the time of conversion, covens often utilize some type of rebirth imagery in the final phase of the initiation ritual. This is especially fitting in Paganism, which acknowledges and celebrates the eternal cycles of life, death, and rebirth found in creation. If you recall the story of my own initiation from Chapter 1, I was asked to squat in a fetal position, then emerge from under a dark cloth to symbolize my spiritual rebirth.

After the initiation ritual is complete, the initiate is considered a full member of the coven or tradition into which he or she was initiated, and will usually take his/her place within the circle for participation in the rest of the rites that have been planned for the evening.

Adopting and Using Craft Names

It is a Pagan custom for newcomers to choose a Craft name, a name that reflects their spiritual selves, and by which they will be known in Pagan circles. Sometimes one name will be chosen for the period of study that mirrors the status of the student, and a different name adopted at initiation. Children born in Craft families will sometimes be given a Craft name at birth, and then be expected to change it when they come of age. Ashleen O'Gaea, in her *Family Wicca Book,* tells of her twelve-year-old son's decision to adopt the name The Explorer. In an article she wrote on vision-quest initiation that appeared several years later in Chas S. Clifton's *Witchcraft Today: Book Three,* she refers to the same child as her teenage son, Questor.

In my experience, Witches change Craft names at least once during their lifetimes, usually in response to a period of growth or to new spiritual interests. Some might have two or three names, a different one having been chosen for each tradition into which she or he has been initiated.

How Craft names are chosen and adopted, how flexible they are to change, and what types of names are deemed appropriate varies from coven to coven. Some covens ask that Craft names never be uttered outside of the circle; in others, members use them when addressing one another wherever and whenever they meet. Still other covens ask that you never reveal your chosen name to anyone but the deities.

In Clan Eireannach we always used our Craft names when addressing one another in ritual situations, and usually kept doing so whenever we were together outside the circle. We grew so accustomed to these names that they became second nature, a true reflection of our inner selves. One woman in our coven liked her Craft name so well that she legally adopted it. I have used mine for so long, and am called by it by so many people both in and out of the Craft, that I have frequently considered doing the same.

There are a wide variety of Craft names to choose from, and many sources from which to seek guidance. Sometimes a Craft name reflects a skill the Witch possesses, or expresses an appreciation for a special part of nature. A Craft name may be the name of a patron deity. The following are all examples of typical Craft names: Willow RainWater, Harvest, Cerridwen Sundancer, Thor Hammerslayer, Lark Firefall, Athena MoonSpinner, Melusine, Jade Myrtlewort, Spinner HeartSong.

Not all Witches take a surname, but many do. Sometimes a Craft surname will reflect the tradition followed by the coven. When I was living in Illinois I knew of a coven called "The Coven of the Silver Moon" whose members all adopted "Silvermoon" as their Craft surname.

In Clan Eireannach we adopted both public and secret Craft names, the public ones usually based on a combination of Irish deity names and Celtic surnames. Most of us took a first name from Irish mythology and a last name that was reflective of our own Celtic heritage, or one whose clan history or motto we loved. Considering that the Irish made up the largest immigrant group to North America, we all found we had several family names to choose from when considering our Craft surnames. Even with this heritage to look back on, not everyone chose a name from their family tree. One man took the surname O'Neill because he was drawn to the legends about this powerful Ulster clan.

I am very fond of the surname I came into this incarnation with, and am proud of its place in history. However, it did nothing for me as a Craft name. Taking with me a list of my Irish family names from as far back as I could trace, I went to the library, planning to spend an afternoon in the reference section looking up as many clan histories as I could find. I began with the clan of my Grandmother McCoy. The McCoys can trace their clan back to the Isle of Iona in the Scottish Hebrides. Iona was one of the last strongholds of Paganism in Scotland, famous for its Druidic center. In the sixth century, St. Columba came to the island and "Christianized" it, and today it is the focus of Christian pilgrimages. Not all the clans on Iona were pleased by this turn of events, and many refused to adopt the new religion even in pretense. The McCoys were one of these clans, and they fled to Ireland in order to keep their Pagan faith. When I finished reading the entry, I closed the book and left the library knowing I had found my perfect Craft surname.

We also adopted secret Craft names in Clan Eireannach, a middle name so to speak, that we dedicated privately to our deities, and that no one but the deities ever knew. How, where, and why this name was chosen was a private matter for the one selecting it, and its selection process was never discussed with others.

The Nature of Craft Ritual

In the following ritual, and in any other Craft rites you are likely to read, you will note that symbolism has a prominent, though sometimes subtle, place. All Wiccan/Pagan rituals, whether solitary or group, rely heavily on symbolism to forge a link between ourselves and the divine. This archetypal, or pattern, language speaks to us without words. For example, lighting a candle in the darkness tells our deep minds that we believe the light of truth chases away the dark of ignorance; turning our five-pointed pentagrams up so that the point representing the divine is over and above those of matter tells us that we are seeking the spiritual rather than the mundane.

Covens have special problems and advantages when working with symbols. On one hand, the ritual has to be constructed so that the symbolic language is meaningful to everyone. On the other hand, covens have the creative input of many people to help craft these archetypes into the ritual in unique ways. For instance, ritual dramas rife with symbolic actions have become popular with covens over the past decade. This opportunity for interactive symbolism, in which each individual part plays off the others to weave a picture of the whole, is one not available to the solitary.

Clan Eireannach's Initiation Rite

What follows is the initiation ritual my coven used when initiating newcomers into both our tradition and our coven. Our tradition is known as Witta, an Irish-based tradition that includes elements of traditional Irish

Paganism and Wicca, with a few Norse Pagan concepts thrown in as well.

Just for the sake of example, we will assume that the initiate in this case is a male. The ritual is the same for either gender. Prior to the ritual, the initiate is expected to spend as much time in reflective solitude as is practical. This period includes a cleansing and purification ritual to be written and performed by the initiate alone. Soon afterwards, his primary teacher (we'll assume she is female for this example) comes to his home to help him dress in his ritual robes and to take him to the meeting site.

To begin the rite, all members of the coven except the initiate and the initiate's primary teacher assemble at the circle site. We cast the circle by drawing it with a wand. Because we are a priestly tradition, the acting leader(s) would be the first to draw the circle by moving clockwise around its perimeter, stopping at each quarter* to evoke its energies. When the entire circle is complete, the rest of the coven members follow around the circle adding their energy to it, and honoring the quarters in any way deemed appropriate by each individual. After that, the acting high priest (AHP) and acting high priestess (AHPS) call upon Lugh and Brighid, the two principal deities of our tradition, to be present and to witness the ritual. In keeping with Celtic tradition, we first offer them food and drink, then light candles in their honor.

---

* Casting the circle, calling the quarters, et cetera, are all skills of basic Witchcraft that lie beyond the scope of this book. Those of you who are Craft newcomers, with no access to a personal teacher, should study books on practical Witchcraft to learn these basics. See the list "Books for Learning More About Basic Witchcraft," page 198 of the appendix, for recommended texts.

After all the preliminaries—as dictated by both Craft custom and the Wittan tradition—are out of the way, the initiation ritual begins. The AHP or AHPS steps to the center of the circle and announces that a young man is this night declaring himself a Witch, that he wishes to enter into the Wittan tradition and be a part of our circle. All this is merely a formality as the man is already known to the coven, having worked with us closely for at least a year.

Our altar sits in the west quarter, and our gateway (the point at which we feel we can safely draw a door in the circle by which to enter and exit) is in the east quarter. These points, too, vary by tradition. The AHP and AHPS walk to the far eastern edge of the circle and ask:

Who wishes to enter this sacred place?

Accompanied by his primary teacher, the initiate walks up to the outside edge of the circle. The initiate is unbound, dressed in his black ritual robe, which is gathered at the waist by the green cord of the student. Green is a symbol of fertility, growth, and newness, and is deemed by our coven an appropriate color for our students to wear throughout their training. Because we are a Celtic-oriented tradition, we value freedom and, like the Celts of old, acknowledge each other as free people when meeting or parting in ritual. For us, binding in any form, not allowing the initiate the free will to change his mind and walk away, is anathema.

Initiate

It is I, (initiate gives his legal name, or the name under which he has been known while a Craft student).

I come with my teacher (gives teacher's Craft name),
who is known to you.

AHP or AHPS
(Teacher's Craft name), *can you vouch for the sincerity of this candidate who stands before us? Is he a learned man?*

Teacher
He has learned much from me and others, and from his own inner self, and yet knows that learning is never ending. I vouch for his knowledge and his sincerity.

AHP or AHPS
The student may be brought to the gateway, but he must cross its threshold alone. No one can pass through the portals between the worlds but by his own will and merit.

The AHP or AHPS cuts a doorway in the circle with a wand, allowing the teacher to enter and take her place in the circle with the rest of the coven. The gateway is then resealed and a broom is placed on the ground at the entry point. This is an old Wiccan custom. The broom is symbolic of the unity of male and female. Stepping over it symbolizes our crossing into the realm of the divine, where male and female have no meaning, but are merely two parts of the whole.

Next, the ordeal begins in the form of a series of questions administered to the initiate. For the most part this is another formality, though the initiate does have to come up with his own answers to the questions. We do this in memory of Lugh, one of our principal deities, who was stopped at the gates of Tara (the stronghold of the Irish

High Kings) and questioned about his skills before he could enter. The initiate is free to answer the questions as he feels best. Whether or not his teacher has counseled him in the answers remains a secret between them.

In general, the questions concern:

- The initiate's qualifications for entering the circle.
- The magickal skills the initiate possesses.
- The contributions the initiate can make to the group.
- Any questions covering basic Craft or Wittan teachings that the coven wishes to ask.

When the questions are answered, the AHP or AHPS looks to the coven for permission to allow the initiate to enter. Since, in this case, the initiation has been planned by all, it is a given that permission will be granted. One of the leaders cuts a door in the gateway and bids the initiate to step inside by crossing over the broom. The doorway is then closed behind him and the broom removed.

AHP or AHPS

Welcome, (state legal or student name), *to this sacred place. In it you stand at the boundary of all worlds, without a firm foothold in any. Here is the world of form and spirit, light and shadow, earth and sky, Otherworld and Earth World. The vows and promises you make here tonight will echo throughout all creation—through past, present, and future; to the upper, middle, and lower worlds. By stepping into this space you show your willingness to make these vows without fear and without hesitation. Are you now ready to begin making these vows by accepting the threefold blessing?*

The threefold blessing is a brief ritual based on the sacred Celtic number three, and uses the imagery of the Triple Goddess—the maiden, mother, and crone (symbolized by the three phases of the moon)—to honor and consecrate the one undergoing the blessing. From the altar a small cauldron is lifted and handed to someone else who will hold it for the AHP and AHPS while the blessing of the salt and water takes place.

Cauldron Bearer

Behold the cauldron of Badb (an Irish crone Goddess who has custody of the great cauldron of life, death, and regeneration in the Otherworld). *To look into its depths is to see all time and space, and to know the unity of our Goddess. From her womb all things are born, and return to it we all must, so that we may be born again as you will be tonight.*

From the altar, the AHPS takes a small silver chalice of water and holds it over the cauldron.

AHPS

Blessed Be the water—the blood of the Goddess from which all life emerges.

The AHPS pours the water into the cauldron. Then the AHP takes a small bowl of salt from the altar and holds it over the cauldron.

AHP

Blessed Be the salt—the body of the Goddess, the Earth Mother who nourishes and sustains us.

The AHP pours the salt into the cauldron. The three coven members who have been selected ahead of time to portray the maiden, mother, and crone Goddess come forward now. They each place a hand into the cauldron and stir the mixture clockwise.

The Three Goddesses
(While stirring) *Water and salt. Blood and earth. Birth, death, and rebirth. I created these. By these I bless those who follow my ways.*

The person portraying the maiden Goddess removes her hand from the cauldron and walks to stand in front of the initiate.

Maiden Goddess
Do you know me?

Initiate
You are the maiden.

The maiden kneels in front of the initiate and touches the salt water to his feet.

Maiden Goddess
I bless your feet that you may always walk the right pathway as you travel this life. May your feet lead you boldly into new ventures and bring you safely home again.

Next, the mother removes her hand from the cauldron and stands in front of the initiate.

Mother Goddess
Do you know me?

Initiate
You are the mother.

The mother places her damp hand low on the initiate's stomach area.

Mother Goddess
I bless your creative center (the words *womb* or *phallus* may be substituted here) *so that fertility shall be inherent in your life's endeavors. May all you touch and hope for that is positive grow and flourish.*

Next, the crone removes her hand from the cauldron and stands in front of the initiate.

Crone Goddess
Do you know me?

Initiate
You are the crone.

The crone places her damp hand on the initiate's forehead.

Crone Goddess
I bless your head that you may have the wisdom to think clearly, love honestly, and always be open to your connection with all that is, was, or ever shall be. For all these things are mine. They came from me, and to me they shall return. Blessed Be that you have returned, my child.

The cauldron is replaced on the altar and the Goddesses withdraw.

The AHP and AHPS now make sure that the initiate is standing in the west end of the circle near the altar and that he is facing the east, a direction symbolic of new beginnings as symbolized in each morning's sunrise.

AHP or AHPS

(Addressing the coven) *The one who stands before us declares himself tonight to be not only a Witch, but he has also declared his intent to share our spiritual path. He wishes to dedicate himself as an initiate of the Wittan tradition. To this end he has studied not only the Witch lore we love, but the teachings of our ways as well. All of you have helped bring him to this place tonight. Accept him, if you will, by welcoming him as a free person.*

Coven

Failte (Irish word meaning "welcome"), (insert legal or student name). *We greet you as a free person.*

AHP

(Addressing initiate) *Do you, this night, of your own free will, declare yourself a Witch?*

Initiate

I am a Witch. I am a Witch. I am a Witch.

AHPS

Do you choose to follow the Wittan tradition of the Craft knowing that, as a free man, you may discard, add to, or combine your spirituality with any other path so long as you harm none?

Initiate

As a free man, and as I harm none, I do what I will.

AHP

As you stand before the Old Ones in this sacred space, do you promise to cherish our ways and respect our beliefs no matter where your spiritual path might lead?

Initiate

I am Wittan. No matter what other labels apply to me, this one shall also stand.

AHPS

Because we know that many of our ways have been lost during the centuries of our oppression, we know that Craft secrets are best not kept forever, that all sincere seekers have a right to these. Therefore we ask you to take the Vow of Nine Years that we all have taken. By this oath you swear to protect and guard the secrets of this coven until the time of darkening balance (Autumn Equinox) *in the common era year* _____ (nine years after the date of this ritual). *Will you make this vow and pledge to us your loyalty in names of the deities you love?*

Initiate

I promise by my God Lugh, and by my Goddess Brighid, that I will love the Wittan path and will protect and guard the secret workings of this coven. If I fail in this promise, may the Law of Three send me justice.

All

As it is spoken, So Mote It Be!

The Law of Three is a Pagan law, better known as the
Threefold Law. It states that any energy directed outward
in any form will be revisited on the sender three times
over. This includes both positive and negative energies.
"So mote it be" is antiquated English traditionally used in
Wiccan covens to mean "so it must be." This statement is
added to spells and rituals just like "Amen" is added to
Judeo-Christian prayers. Both are affirmations that the
thing that has been enacted is a current reality.

AHPS

*Then know this as the first of the great mysteries: In the
spiritual we are all children. We must always continue
to grow or our spirit dies. Never stop learning, for
knowledge is the food of the hungry soul.*

From the altar, the AHP takes a small plate, on which are
small portions of salmon, pork, and a single hazel nut. In
Irish mythology the salmon and the nut are symbols of
great knowledge and of secrets revealed. The pork is
related to the Otherworld feasts of the Gods. The significance of each is explained to the initiate, after which
each portion is fed to him by the AHP.

From the altar, the AHP and AHPS take a thick cord
woven from three smaller cords of white, red, and black.
These are the colors of the Celtic Triple Goddess, chosen
by our coven to replace the discarded green cord of the
student. The new cord contains nine knots, each spaced
a foot apart, symbolizing the power number in Celtic tra-

ditions, the sacred three-times-three. The significance of the cord is explained to the initiate, though this is merely a formality since the initiate made the cord himself in order to infuse it with his own energies. After the explanation, the initiate's primary teacher steps forward to remove the green cord from around his waist.

Teacher

A good teacher is also taught by her student. I cherish what I learned from you, and am honored to bring you here this night because of what you learned from me. It is every teacher's hope that her students will surpass her. This is my fervent wish for you, my friend.

The initiate and student may wish to hug or express other sentiments to each other either aloud or in whispers. The teacher will keep the green cord for her student to reclaim after the initiation to do with it what he wills. Some wish to keep them as magical talismans, others burn or bury them.

The persons who are portraying the Triple Goddess come forward again and tie the cord around the initiate's waist. This is usually done by centering it across the stomach, pulling each end behind the initiate's back, where it crosses, then bringing it back around to the front, where it is tied.

Our use of the cord is largely ceremonial, but in the Pagan past these cords were used to magickally protect a coven from a traitor. Some covens today still practice this custom, called "taking one's measure." The cord is measured to the exact length of the initiate and then magickally linked to that person, either through ritual or by having his blood, hair, nail clippings, or some personal token tied up in the cord. In the past the cord was retained by the coven so that it could be turned against the initiate magickally should he betray the coven to the authorities. Today it is retained as a sign of unity.

After the cord has been tied around the initiate, the women of Clan Eireannach form a line facing east. They stand one behind the other with legs spread.

AHP and AHPS
(Last use of initiate's legal or student name inside a Wittan circle), *go and be reborn.*

The initiate starts at the west end of the line of women and crawls between their legs in a symbolic act of rebirthing. He moves from the west, the direction of the Otherworld from which all things are reborn, to the east, the direction of new beginnings. This is a joyous and fun event, as everyone tries to execute this maneuver with long robes and cords dangling in the way. When the initiate emerges at the other end of the line, the men are the first to greet him with hugs and shouts of joy. Then the women join them, all welcoming the new Witch and new Wittan to the coven.

As soon as order can be restored, the new Witch goes to the altar, where he stands alone to make his personal dedication to Lugh and Brighid. He is also free to acknowledge other personal deities he may have. At this time he states his chosen Craft name aloud so that the rest of the coven can hear what it is. This is the name he will be known by from this point on. The initiate also takes his private Craft name, the one that will be known only by the deities. It is our tradition that it be taken at this time, in silence.

When the initiate is finished, he faces the coven members, who greet him by his new Craft name and welcome him again to the coven, the Craft, and to the Wittan tradition, acknowledging him as a free person.

After this, the new Witch takes his place in the circle for his first experience of the inner-circle rituals. Many covens have such secret rituals. Ours included Irish ritual magick techniques that we developed ourselves, though they were based on common occult and magickal practices, and similar practices can no doubt be found in other covens.

After the ritual is complete, we thank our deities, dismiss the quarters, and close our circle with the traditional Wiccan words of parting: "Merry meet, merry part, and merry meet again!"

After the ritual, we usually go out and treat our new member to a celebration. It is a time to celebrate accomplishments and rejoice in our unity.

And that's it: a typical coven initiation ritual. Different in content, but similar in form to most others. No human sacrifice, no use of bloody animal entrails, no swearing of allegiance to anti-Gods. Just a moving and joyful experience for welcoming newcomers to the circle in which the divine and its creation are honored and celebrated.

Chapter 6

PERFECT LOVE
and
PERFECT TRUST

By LONG-STANDING TRADITION, Witches' covens are instructed to meet in an atmosphere of perfect love and perfect trust. Just when this injunction became a commonly accepted goal is open for debate, but through the writings of some of the pioneers of the modern Craft movement we know that the teaching dates *at least* as far back as late nineteenth-century Europe, though it may actually be many centuries older than this. This teaching has confused Witches, and has raised many impossible-to-meet expectations for new covens and new coven members, which often end up causing frustrations that threaten the life of the group.

The teaching of perfect love and perfect trust is a model not only for the circle, but for living. It implies acceptance of all people, with their faults and strengths. Inside a coven it is the highest goal we are asked to achieve, an expression of our faith in each other as microcosms of the divine. It is also an expression of our relationship to the divine, that we love our Gods and Goddesses, trust in their power, and trust in the power they gave to us.

Instant intimacy is a lie. Perfect love and perfect trust do not happen just because a circle is cast; they must be nurtured. Just because someone shares your ritual space does not mean you must instantly love and trust this person, no matter how much you may wish to. All good relationships start slowly. Think back to your first meeting with your best friend. What can you remember about it? What were your first impressions? How did these change over time? How long did it take you to start doing things together by yourselves? How long before you were able to share secrets and know they would go no further? How long before you knew this person would sacrifice time and energy—or maybe his/her life—on your behalf? Chances are that, no matter how great your beginning, there was a gradual building of love and trust. So it is with a coven.

The Pitfalls of Forced Intimacy

In response to this confusion over perfect love and perfect trust, some covens have created rituals to test these tenets among their members, especially when a new member joins a group. One of the by-products of this thinking is the ordeal by terror and/or pain mentioned in Chapter 5. The misguided leader in such covens wants newcomers to prove that they feel loved enough to trust that the leader will pull back at the last moment and not deliver that final killing blow. Enduring such rituals are not proof of anyone's love and trust, and I have neither seen nor heard of a situation in which these overt displays of sadism helped to build either. Quite the opposite usually occurs. Resentments begin building over the procedure that eventually manifest as challenges to the power structure of the coven.

Some covens use perfect love and perfect trust as the basis for their decision to worship skyclad. They believe that when people are at their most vulnerable (i.e., naked) that they are proving their trust in the rest of the group. While this may be true between people who have known and worked together for a long time, it becomes no more than a test of nerves for new covens or new coven members. Nudity among strangers may measure how badly someone wishes to join a group, but it is not proof of trust or love.

Other covens try to force bonding by taking their cues from the encounter group craze of the early 1970s, when groups of strangers met for weekend seminars in which trust exercises were a main feature. One of the favorite disciplines was to have an individual stand inside the circle of strangers attending the seminar. Holding his or her arms stiffly across the chest, the individual would fall backwards into the circle to be passed around like a giant log. This faith that the rest of the circle would not let the person fall was supposed to show his or her trust in the others. I have never been sure what this was supposed to accomplish in the long run, since having that sort of faith in strangers in the real world is not only silly, but dangerous. These encounter groups also encouraged strangers to bare their innermost feelings and fears to each other in order to prove that they would still be loved. To underscore the point, group hugging after these painful and private revelations was the norm.

What the proponents of these encounters failed to realize was that the type of love and trust that sustains groups of persons who know each other intimately cannot exist between strangers. A stranger can love and respect you for your humanness, or for your willingness to share certain experiences with him/her, but someone who does not truly know you on all levels of being cannot love or trust you deeply enough to merge their personal energies with your own. This more profound type of bonding is essential for a coven to work magick and ritual together.

The Problem with Trusting Too Soon

Remember that it takes time for members of new groups to get relaxed enough to become completely at ease with each other. It may take months for a person's true personality to come shining through, and you may get a few surprises, some good, some not so pleasant. On the plus side, that shy flower who never ever thought she could lead a ritual may blossom into a natural priestess in a loving, trusting environment. On the minus side, that amicable fellow who always has a ready smile for everyone might turn out to be a backstabber who thinks he should take over the coven for the good of everyone.

One of my pre-Clan Eireannach covens experienced a miserable disturbance when someone deliberately broke the sacred bonds of trust. The group had not been together very long, and our bonding process was slowed by people moving out of the area, or by work schedules that were not coven-friendly. The only thing I felt we really had going for us was a solid core of five members. I was starting to feel very good about knowing these people. Having reached the initial trust stage, one of our members, Sharon, confided her arachnophobia (fear of spiders) to us. Knowing that we all fear something, tangible or not, we sympathized, but did not dwell on her problem.

On the night of our next full moon ritual, one of the coven members (I'll just refer to him as "BadWitch") showed up on my doorstep with a small box containing his pet tarantula. Immediately Sharon's phobia was in my mind. Since the ritual was at my home, and I was the coven's priestess, I did not hesitate to tell BadWitch to please put the spider's box in the dining room before Sharon saw it. As we all began gathering up our equipment to carry out to stone circle in the back yard, I forgot about the spider, assuming it was safely out of sight in the dining room.

We began the ritual and were preparing to Draw Down the Moon (see Chapter 8), when BadWitch suddenly produced the tarantula—sans box—in front of everyone. Naturally Sharon was terrified. BadWitch began to wax poetically about the spider as a symbol of the Goddess, the creatrix who spins all things into the creation.

All of us were well aware of these associations, but were more aware of Sharon struggling valiantly to keep her composure. A phobia is not a rational fear, but a blown-all-out-of-proportion hysteria, and people have been known to actually drop dead when unexpectedly faced with their phobia.

BadWitch was casting sly grins in Sharon's direction as he toyed with the spider, announcing that unless we proved we could handle the creature, we were not fit to have the Goddess drawn down into us. Every one of us knew that Sharon had been chosen to be the vessel of the Goddess that night, and that BadWitch's pronouncement was meant for her.

For a few moments all was silent. None of us could believe that a trusted member of our coven would stoop to such pointless cruelty. Knowing that it was my responsibility to handle the situation, I said a quick prayer to Brighid for help.

Just then, whether by design or accident I will never know for sure, BadWitch dropped the creature on the ground. Naturally, it made a made wild dash on all eight hairy legs straight for Sharon. I have always rather enjoyed having spiders around the house, but I have to admit that watching this uninvited, fist-sized guest scurrying across our circle was unsettling.

Unable to contain herself any longer, Sharon screamed and, in her terror, toppled our altar as she ran out of the circle without bothering to cut a door for safe passage. As the quarters had already been called and our ritual energies raised, this break in our protection put us all at risk. Meanwhile BadWitch went scrambling after his pet, which was in danger of being crushed by falling ritual tools and stampeding feet.

My dog, aroused by all the commotion, stood at the patio door barking madly. Sharon ran towards the house, threw the patio door open, and flung herself inside, forgetting about the screen door, which was still in place. The screen tore loose, its ripping sound audible in what was left of the circle. The momentary resistance of the screen caused her to lose her balance, and she stumbled over the surprised dog and hit her head on the breakfast bar.

All this chaos happened in less than two minutes, but the damage done was lasting. I sent BadWitch and his pet packing, and with the menacing glare of the others backing me up, he didn't argue. He muttered something about us being poor excuses for Witches, then left.

BadWitch violated not only our trust but our sacred space as well, by making sure that it was not a safe space for Sharon. He defiled the sacred energies, our deities, and put everyone at risk of psychic attack by causing a break in the circle.

Unbelievably, he still considered himself part of the coven. We thought he was gone for good, but at our next full moon he showed up at my front door—without the spider—ready to work. Sharon said nothing, but another member walked out, refusing to step into sacred space with him again.

Later, we all met without BadWitch to discuss the problem. We decided that the breech of basic trust had gone too far. The decision, reached with difficulty, was banishment (see Chapter 11). This was the only coven of which I have been a part in which such a drastic step had to be taken, and I hope I never have to endure it again.

In our efforts to keep our coven functioning amidst people coming and going, we allowed ourselves to trust BadWitch too soon. If we had known him better, perhaps we would have known him to be a petty person who enjoyed feeling personally powerful at another's expense.

Another downfall of trusting too soon is in repeating rituals or practices that are not ethical, but that everyone has grown used to and accepts as right. This is especially true when younger, less confident Witches are in covens with unscrupulous people who are more bent on inflating their egos and personal power than in doing anything spiritual. At only one coven meeting have I witnessed a horror scene so bad that I couldn't believe what I was seeing. I was only a circle guest, and was able to walk away, but I have worried for years over those fearful young people who all did as they were told, and seemed unaware that they were being led into dangerous areas that had nothing to do with Witchcraft.

Weaving the Ties That Bind

If you are in the right group for you, the members of your circle will eventually become your extended family, and some of the best friends you could ever have will be found within its perimeter. Time is the best way to build up the kind of perfect love and perfect trust you want, but meanwhile there are things you can do to help foster feelings of intimacy without turning your coven into an encounter group.

I have found that doing things as a group is a good start. This does not mean meeting for ritual situations. Keep to your agreed-upon ritual schedule and the group mind you create will certainly help forge your ties to one another. When I speak of "doing things" together, however, I am talking about doing non-Witchy things as a group.

When Clan Eireannach first formed, we found that we all got along amazingly well. Our personal energies blended smoothly, and we shared similar views on many issues, both secular and spiritual. This was great for our worship and magickal situation, but was doing nothing to foster deeper friendships among us. Eventually someone suggested that the twelve of us move outside of our circle and venture together into the real world. Of course we all enthusiastically agreed in principle. Then came the problem of logistics.

Biddy and I liked folk art and craft shows, Sionnan loved live rock concerts, Bran was strictly into classical music and bowling, but Mollie and Dana were into country music and folk festivals. Holly played soccer and haunted art museums. Niamh hated all museums, but liked the garden and home shows that Finn despised. Dana and I liked going to the Broadway series at a downtown theater, while Tari was into amusement parks and baseball. Mollie, Biddy, and I liked talking late into the night at coffee shops. Bran and Liban were strictly into eat-and-run fast food. To make it worse, the members of our coven were scattered over south and southeastern Texas to the point that it was a two-hour drive between some of our homes. Impossible, right?

Almost, but not quite.

After every full moon, when we were all relaxed and snacking together, we threw out suggestions for things we could do together in the month to come. The point was to get to know each other better as individuals, so unless someone in the group really loathed an idea, anything that most of us could clear our schedules to attend was fair game.

As a group, we attended the San Antonio Stock Show and Rodeo and the Texas Renaissance Festival. We went to a midnight bowl-a-thon, spent a weekend at the beach in Port Aransas, did dinner theater and dog shows, did some bargain hunting in Mexico, and went antiquing in beautiful downtown Fredericksberg. We also involved our mates/spouses and children whenever we could to further build our extended family connection.

We all took some good-natured teasing about our personal favorites, especially when things failed to go smoothly, such as when it rained during our entire weekend on a Padre Island beach. However, even in the unexpected we were able to find ways to forge our bonds. Twenty-five-plus adults and children crammed into three condos for a rainy weekend could have been disastrous, but creative games, guided meditations, and an impromptu "blessed be the rain" ritual on a deserted stretch of beach only strengthened our ties and provided us with a solid base of shared memories to reflect back on later.

After a few months we began to instinctively know one another's tastes. We could look at an item in a shop and confidently say, "Oh look, you know so-and-so would love that." We began to choose events to attend that we knew would please others in the group, willing to sacrifice our own interests to make another person happy. We had become a family.

Being out together as a family enabled us to experience all of the advantages our ancestors had in their clan/kin-group living arrangements. It certainly helped to have a dozen extra pairs of adult eyes at the zoo when the kids all wanted to race off in different directions, and it was nice that everyone could help chip in with driving duties, bringing picnic supplies, cooking food, and cleaning up. We all had our assigned tasks at each outing, and learned to trust each other to fulfill these, from childcare to wiping down picnic tables.

Another way we built our group ties was by meeting outside of the circle for seasonal parties to which we invited not just our families, but also friends who were sympathetic to our religion, though perhaps not a part of it. For three years my husband and I and another Craft couple not in Clan Eireannach co-hosted a Samhain party at our home to which members of both our covens, other friends, and potential Craft students were invited. The bonding that went on at these gatherings was phenomenal, and I still reminisce fondly about these parties with those who were there.

As with any family, you will come to rely on each person's individual strengths, and you will discover each other's insecurities, weakness, and faults. Learning to accept these as part of the total package of someone you care for is necessary for any relationship to flourish, particularly one as intimate as a coven. You will learn not only to have perfect love and trust, but to appreciate each other's talents and overlook each other's failings.

All of this closeness translates perfectly into your coven's ritual work. Crafting rituals that go beyond mere form and words becomes much easier when you are all friends. For instance, when we needed someone to portray a specific deity for one of our lavish Irish ritual magick events, there was no argument over parts, sometimes not even a discussion. Certain personalities just fit, and we all knew it. This intimate knowledge of one another's spiritual make-up not only made our rituals more potent from the standpoint of placing the right person in the right job, but made it a lot easier for us to view the person taking on the persona of the divine in the part for which he or she seemed so perfect.

The days when the members of Clan Eireannach felt they had to work at being together blended seamlessly into a time when it was just as natural as being with one's own family. Thanks to those early efforts, a sense of personal comfort came to all of us—the kind that makes you feel you can call someone up just to chat, go out for coffee or to the movies, or hash over personal problems. To fall back on an old cliché that rings so true, there was not one person in the coven we all wouldn't have trusted with our lives. When Mollie was diagnosed with breast cancer in 1988, that is precisely what happened. All of the magickal energies of the coven were thrown into strengthening her. I believe that one of the reasons our efforts worked as well as they did for as long as they did was that we loved her, and she trusted us to do our best for her.

Perfect love and perfect trust.

Chapter 7

COVEN MAGICK

and

HEALING RITUALS

WITCHES BELIEVE IN MAGICK. We do more than believe in it. We accept our ability to act as a channel through which magickal energy can be magnified, focused, and directed. We use our own minds, our bodies, and those forces that nature provides to accomplish our goals. Magick is not evil. It is not even supernatural. Nothing supernatural can exist. All matter acts in accordance with the laws of the universe. Science has named some of those laws for us. Others, like those that drive magickal operations, are still waiting to be discovered—but they clearly exist. It is a truth that the magick of yesterday is the science of today, just as today's magick will be the science of tomorrow.

Because Witches have accepted the use of magick as their right, and have been successful, they have been feared. Displays of power always inspire fear from the dominant classes of any society. This fear was, and likely still is, at the base of the Witch persecutions.

A Witch with magickal power is not a proverbial loose cannon, zapping anybody within striking range. Witchcraft is a religion, therefore governed by ethics. At its heart is our Rede: As it harms none, we do what we will. Our use of power is limited to positive actions only. The penalty for violating this ethic is the Threefold Law, another manifestation of natural power that returns to us three times over any energy we direct outward.

It is true that not all Witches behave ethically at all times. Do all Christians, all Jews, all Moslems? Like the followers of other religions, we are only human. Most Witches try to live up to the teachings of their faith, otherwise they wouldn't be following a religion at all. They would just be out there slinging negativity any which way they wanted.

The Basics of Coven Spell-Crafting

Newcomers to the Craft are anxious to learn about magick, particularly the powerful magickal workings of covens. Often they are surprised to discover that Witches do not belong to the "Spell of the Day Club," and that magick is used sparingly by many groups and individuals. Our primary function is worship. Magick is merely a by-product of that worship, one of the tools our faith gives us to use when needed. We see our deities as manifest in all creation; therefore, when we connect with nature we are able to draw on its divine energy to craft magick. Casting spells without the aid of the divine is certainly possible, but more difficult and unpredictable.

In recent years there has been a lot of coverage in the New Age press about the power of the individual will. Even modern medicine has started taking advantage of these same visualization and self-will techniques to help speed the healing processes, and the results are encouraging. One of the reasons coven magick is so potent is that it takes the individual wills of several spiritually close people and blends them into one colossal group will. This group mind, when trained in the magickal arts and focused on a single goal, can indeed produce awe-inspiring results.

While will is important to magick, by tradition several other conditions are required for successful spell-crafting. These are:

- The need.
- The desire.
- The knowledge.
- The silence.

We must truly need what we ask for, be it healing, money, protection, et cetera. We also must have a desire for the magickal goal, the more obsessive the better, for this is the emotion that drives the will. The requirement of desire is one reason covens hesitate to work spells on behalf of people they do not know well. While they may be sympathetic to the situation, it is hard to work up a good obsession over a secondhand story about someone else's need.

We must also possess the knowledge of how magick works, and of the elements needed to construct an effective spell for a desired goal.

The last requirement, silence, is an ancient custom that teaches us to keep our magickal needs and efforts to ourselves. An old Witch saying tells us that "energy shared is energy lost." Your energy should be going towards your goal, not channeled into idle chatter about it. Another reason to keep silent is to prevent doubters, or others who have a vested interest in your failure, from counteracting your work.

Because the magick of the coven is more potent than that of the individual, the stakes are higher and the repercussions for the misuse of power more intense. Like solitary Witches, wise covens will use divination to ascertain the outcome of any spell before it is worked. Some covens ask all members to do their favorite divination in private and report the results back to the group. Others might have one "officer" who is gifted in divination routinely perform this operation on behalf of the group.

In Clan Eireannach, we decided that since we were going to do the spell as a group, we should perform the divination as a group. The precise method we used varied according to who was chosen to be the principal seer at each divination event. That person would incorporate into the ritual the methods she or he was most skilled in using. Naturally, those who read patterns in the sky or the ritual fire produced a more dramatic sideshow than those of us who used tarot cards or runes, but the end product was still reliably the same. I remember one divination during which the chosen seer was using the bonfire to induce visions when, for no reason we could discern, the fire literally leaped dramatically upward at the very moment the answers came clear to the seer.

In order to get an accurate divination a spell must be fully constructed ahead of time, with all visualizations, wording, tools, and catalysts (herbs, stones, et cetera) completely outlined. It is especially important with a group spell that certain aspects of the visualization process be agreed upon in advance. How the goal is to be visualized says a lot about who the spell will affect and how they will be affected. Visualization, the mental seeing of the end result, is the primary tool through which spells are empowered. The power is in the mind of the Witch, not in the instruments that are used.

Differences between Solitary and Group Magick

When an individual Witch sets out to create a spell, he or she usually consults the spellbook and decides what type of catalyst will work best: a candle spell, a stone spell, one using special herbs, et cetera. She or he will spend lots of time picking out color correspondences or looking up sympathetic deities to call on for assistance. The spell is then worked at least once, although usually it is repeated several nights in succession, until the practitioner feels it has "taken."

Intense, clear visualization of the goal and the raising of energy, which are basic to all spellwork, may be done without the Witch ever getting up from a sitting position in front of his/her altar. Certainly the option to raise energy by more kinetic means is there, but many solitaries prefer to use only their minds as instruments of power to charge the stone, herbs, or other objects with magickal intent.

Covens may not be able to meet several nights in succession to re-work a spell. Time commitments or distances just don't make this a practical option in most cases. A spell is worked once, then often not re-evaluated by the group for another full lunar month. Usually, but not always, covens forgo all of the corresponding accouterments, such as herbs known to have an affinity for the goal, and focus solely on making magick through the efforts of visualization and raising and sending energy through very physical means.

How Covens Raise Magickal Energy

To perform any act of magick, energy must be raised, focused, and directed. The energy that fuels magick is naturally occurring, but our ability to feel, raise, and use it must be achieved with practice. Perhaps early in human history, when people lived more in tune with the rhythms of nature, using this energy came naturally. For today's followers of earth religions, covens provide some of the best teachers of this ancient skill.

I know of one new Witch who was studying to join the coven of a friend of mine. He had learned to draw in energy on his own, though it was sadly uncontrolled. He decided he was more gifted than the rest of the group because he was constantly drawing in so much energy that he had to stop several times a day and throw himself into a tripod position just to ground it all. Eventually he left the group in a huff, claiming that he was the only real

Witch among them. What he didn't stick around long enough to learn was that leaving himself open to collecting random energies is not Witchcraft. Witchcraft is just what the term implies—a craft, an art. If he had stayed with the coven for his full year and a day of training, he would have learned how to control how much energy he took in, and also discovered that grounding the excess did not require actually touching the earth. It can be done discreetly through the feet or root chakra (the energy center at the base of your spine) even while sitting in an airplane at 35,000 feet!

The energy raised for magick comes either from Mother Earth, and is visualized as being drawn up from below, or from the divine, and is visualized as being drawn down from above. To help us focus on raising that energy, covens usually employ one or a combination of methods involving sound or movement. Dancing, drumming, singing, chanting, and rhythmic breathing, are all popular choices.

While all this is taking place, the energy within the circle begins to build and is formed into a cohesive pattern by the clear intent of the coven. As much as the ritual circle is created to protect the Witches within from outside invasion, it is also in place to contain this raised energy until it is ready to be sent out. Even the novice Witch can easily feel this power growing in the circle. In a coven whose members are skilled at raising energy it is not uncommon to see some confirmation of the effort. Static electricity, St. Elmo's Fire, and increased air temperature may all be evident. The power manifests physically with nervous tension, elevated blood pressure, and increased respiration and heartbeat.

The energy raised by a coven in the circle is commonly referred to as the Cone of Power. This is seen as a swirling mass of energy, peaking over the circle like an inverted tornado. The Cone will be swirling in a clockwise rotation for spells needing the energy of increase or gain, and in a counter-clockwise direction for spells needing the energy of decrease or loss.

Popular superstition about counter-clockwise movements in the circle has colored the way some newcomers react to using this motion. There has been a prevalent belief that all magick done clockwise is inherently good, and all magick done counter-clockwise is inherently evil. Here is another "mystery" of the Craft revealed: good and evil are not native to either motion. In general, Pagan theology and cosmology do not recognize clear-cut divisions between what is good and what is wicked. Power is power. Only the intent of the Witch decides in which camp the spell falls. For instance, a spell worked with clockwise motions to bring on an illness is certainly negative, while one worked counter-clockwise to banish a bad habit is positive. In the latter case, the magick is of a destructive nature, but it has plainly positive results.

The leader of the coven is the person usually responsible for determining when the energy level has reached its peak, the highest point to which it can build before it begins to wane. At this point, she or he signals everyone to halt their efforts. Quickly, a clear visualization of the intent of the spell, or of the person to whom the energy must be sent, is made, and then the Cone is sent on its way.

Sending out the Cone of Power most often involves a combination of visualization and physical gestures, usually whichever amalgamation the individual members feel best represents to their group mind the image of energy spent. In Clan Eireannach we were fond of lifting and slinging the Cone while spinning outward. Exhaling, throwing up the arms, collapsing on the ground, turning outward as a group, yelling the cone away, lifting it with the arms, shouting, flinging it—any of these methods are good. They work the same way all magick works—because the Witch believes.

The Sacred Art of Healing

Take one look into any old magickal grimoire from any land or culture and you will be struck by the preponderance of spells and charms used for curing everything from warts to the plague. Not surprisingly, these are the spells that have best survived through the years of persecution. They were the magicks that the common people knew worked, and that they refused to let go even under threat of death.

Witches have always been healers. It is one of our most important magicks. Some are more gifted in this arena than others, but it remains one of our most basic practices. We can trace this tradition back to the village wise woman and cunning man of Europe, the granny woman of Appalachia, and the conjure man of Latin America. All of these solitary figures were, and sometimes still are, sought out for healing. They know how to raise and direct healing energies, and which herbs and plants can be distilled into medicines to back up these magickal efforts.

There is an old saying among Pagans: one cannot know how to cure unless one knows how to kill. The energies used are the same. They are part of the universal power that animates all life. Knowing how to manipulate them, coupled with a commitment to the ethical use of will, makes the only difference between so-called white and black magick. Knowing that the same village Witch who dispensed healing could also dispense illness and death is another fear that drove the Witch hunters, and took medicine out of the hands of the Pagans and into the halls of a medical science that has always denied the power of nature and the individual to heal.

Getting Permission to Heal

Pagan ethics teach us that all people are responsible for their own well-being. This is not to imply that people are sick because they want or deserve to be ill. Such thinking is dangerous; it leads us to a blame-the-victim mentality that can rob us of our compassion and our sense of justice. Once we do fall ill, we have the right to decide for ourselves whether we will accept healing treatments, what kind, for how long, and from whom. Because of this, it has always been a Pagan custom to obtain the person's express permission for a healing ritual to take place. Anything less is a violation of free will, a slap on the face of our Rede.

This need for permission can be upsetting for someone who comes to a coven asking for a healing on behalf of a loved one who will not give permission, either from lack of belief or because he or she simply is choosing to refuse all treatment. I had to turn down such requests myself on behalf of our coven, and the response it provokes can get ugly. I have been screamed at, threatened, and called names I would rather not repeat. When this happens, it is best just to keep your cool and walk away. No amount of explaining your position will ease anger born of fear for a loved one.

The Source of Healing Energy

I am occasionally asked by both Pagans and non-Pagans if healing magick doesn't wear me out, sap my strength, and put me at risk of acquiring the very illness I am seeking to drive out of someone else. The answer is—NO!

Here is another of those great "mysteries" of the Craft: The energy with which you heal is not your own. You are merely a channel or medium for it, a means of focusing and directing the power. Like the energy used in the spellwork mentioned earlier in this chapter, the energies raised for healing are drawn either from Mother Earth or from the universal divine. As with any magickal operation, healing is work, and it takes effort to make it happen. If you are doing it right, when it is over you should feel the same way you do after a vigorous aerobic workout. You know you have expended effort, you are a bit fatigued from your exertion, but you are also wonderfully invigorated.

Healing magick can be done from a remote location, either by having the coven send the energy in the form of the Cone of Power or by having skilled members of the coven send their consciousness out from their physical bodies to personally administer to someone not at the ritual site.

Having the person who needs the healing present is, of course, the easiest and most direct way to heal. When the ill person sits at the center of the circle, she or he sits at the intersection of all time and space, making it easy to open up to the curative energies being channeled in from both the earth and the universal divine. The visualizations of the coven can be backed up with hands-on efforts that always make the healing energies stronger.

The custom of "the laying on of hands" in order to transfer spiritual, magickal, or healing forces is almost as old as humanity itself, and the practice can be found in almost all spiritual systems. Of all of our coven's healing rituals, none was more successful or important to us than the ones we did for Mollie, our anchor. Nearly all of these used the hands-on approach. In 1988 she was diagnosed with a particularly aggressive form of breast cancer. The original prognosis was that she would not live another six months. Her positive attitude and our healing rituals prolonged her life and kept up its quality for another two-and-a-half years.

Healing rituals can and should be tailored to meet the needs of the person who is sick. For example, if the person is in need of having toxins removed from his/her body, the energy channeled might come from directly over the sick person, then be pushed out through the feet and grounded in Mother Earth. If the problem is a sick child the energy might need to be playful, to ease the child's fears and encourage his/her own innate healing energies to emerge.

One of the members of Clan Eireannach, Liban, had a four-year-old son named Brandon who began having nightmares after one of his favorite uncles died of leukemia. At his age, no amount of reassurance about the Summerland (a Wiccan version of heaven), reincarnation, or the eternal nature of the soul was going to make sense. Only empirical evidence of these truths was going to help ease him through the period of adjustment, and we had no way to provide this. To make matters worse, when he asked Liban why his uncle died, she answered without thinking, saying, "He got sick." When the child came down with the flu a few months later he was inconsolable. It didn't take us long to realize why. The harm was already done, and the only thing we could do was work on damage control until Brandon was a little older and his mother could re-explain death to him in a more positive manner.

Brandon trusted his mother and, more importantly, he trusted in her magick, because he had seen evidence that it worked. A healing ritual done in a way a child could appreciate and accept would calm his fears. We all met at Liban's house under the guise of a friendly visit. Brandon was not improving, and his fears were not allowing his body's natural healing abilities to go to work for him. Pretending that it was an afterthought, someone suggested a healing ritual to drive the sickness away. Since that's what we had come to do in the first place, we all readily agreed. We were lucky that our patient was only four or he would have easily seen through our ruse. When his permission was granted, we went to work.

To keep things simple and non-threatening we did not bring along any tools, but relied on our imaginations to inspire us in the right direction. We did a silly dance to raise the energy, one that actually got Brandon laughing, and we called out silly threats to the illness to drive it out.

We playfully tickled the boy to make the sickness flee. This also allowed us to make contact long enough to transfer the energy we were raising to him. In spite of our silliness, he trusted us to help him, and he soon began to improve.

Clan Eireannach's Basic Healing Ritual

In our coven we used a simple method of energy transference to heal those who came into our circle for assistance, similar to what we did for Brandon.

After the circle was cast and all preliminaries were complete, the person needing the healing took his or her place in the center of the circle. The AHP or AHPS asked again if the person truly wanted the healing. Once permission was granted, we all worked together to raise as much energy in the circle as possible. Dancing while chanting or singing was our favorite method, and everyone was free to draw energy up from the earth or down from above as they felt best.

When the acting leader decreed that the energy in the circle had peaked, the rest of the coven moved to the center to form a tight circle around the person. We wanted to be close enough to place our dominant hands (the ones we write with) on the head of the sick person. We turned our non-dominant hands either up or down, depending on the direction from which we were drawing our energy. In this way we prepared to become channels for the life force, the divine energy that is in and of all creation.

While this took place, the ill person visualized the sickness flowing from him, being channeled harmlessly into the ground on which he sat. He saw negative energy vacating his body so that the positive, curative energy being raised could take its place inside him.

As the energy flowed through the non-dominant hands, it was directed out through the dominant hands and into the sick person. One member of the group was selected ahead of time to sense when this flow reached its peak, the point at which the visualization could no longer be adequately sustained. At this point we stopped the energy flow and mentally shrouded the ill person in a bath of strengthening, protective white-gold light.

Chapter 8

FESTIVALS, CELEBRATIONS, and OBSERVANCES

THE CYCLES OF THE SEASONS AND THE MOON, and the celebration of life's milestones, are basic parts of Wiccan/Pagan spirituality. We know these cycles as the Wheel of the Year and the Wheel of Life.

You won't find long transcripts of coven rituals in this chapter because I do not feel that these serve the purpose of this book, which is to provide you with ideas for meeting and forming your own coven, and to offer you a glimpse into actual coven life. As anyone who engages in ritual knows, the subtle energies that are raised have to be experienced to be fully understood. Even when one ritual is precisely the same as another on paper, each time it is enacted it is different. The power and intent behind a ritual makes it unique. In a coven, it is the close atmosphere of a spiritual family that makes rituals fulfilling.

Instead of presenting ritual transcripts, which can be found in virtually any book on basic Wiccan/Pagan practice, I have opted to explain the cycles of Wiccan/Pagan spiritual life and give you an idea of how our coven observed some of them.

Celebrating Our Rites of Passage

There are numerous life cycle events celebrated within the Pagan spiritual community. Inside the secure atmosphere of a coven these cycles can have special meaning, especially when your family and friends do not share your spiritual beliefs.

These rites of passage include, but are not limited to:

Wiccaning/Paganing: The dedication of a newborn to the Pagan deities, called either Wiccaning or Paganing, depending on one's tradition.

Coming of Age: A ceremony to initiate a young person into spiritual adulthood, usually at age thirteen for boys and at menarche for girls.

Initiation: The induction of a newcomer into the Craft (see Chapter 5).

Handfasting: Pagan marriage, which may or may not be legally binding.

Handparting: Pagan divorce.

Parenthood: Connected with Wiccaning ceremonies, honoring the initiation of one or two people into the role of parents.

Croning/Elderhood: The celebration and acknowledgment of aging.

Passing-Over: Death and memorial rituals.

All of these life steps are celebrated within covens, but some of them, by their very nature, must involve people outside the group. Therefore, you will quickly find that the example rituals found in Craft books provide only a skeleton on which to flesh out the ritual to personal tastes. Handfasting is a perfect example of this. In many ways, Witch weddings are like any other. There is much nervous anticipation and joy as the couple excitedly works together and with friends and family to come up with unique ways to personalize the ceremony within the framework of their spiritual tradition. Just as weddings in any setting are attended by persons of diverse religious backgrounds, so are Pagan weddings. Families, co-workers, and friends are not all going to be Pagan, any more than they are all going to belong to any other single faith.

Passing-over rituals to memorialize the dead or assist them in making a smooth transition to the Otherworld do not have to be attended solely by the coven. However, because the deceased's family probably did not share his/her faith, these relatives rarely attend a passing-over ritual. Without proper prior planning, a Witch who dies is at the mercy of his/her next of kin as to funeral arrangements, and in most cases is not likely to get a Pagan ritual. Due to these factors, passing-over rites usually take place in a coven after the "real" funeral is over.

Our coven never acknowledged a passing in the same way twice, though due to the repetitive nature of ritual some elements remained the same. Usually we held our rituals as a simple memorial service inside our circle, though sometimes we met at a gravesite or at a place where ashes had been scattered.

As I mentioned in an earlier chapter, rituals are built on symbolism, and there is much to choose from when honoring the dead. We made heavy use of candles, both to symbolize the light of the life force and to illuminate the path to the Otherworld. We cut cords, symbolizing the severing of life, and each member of the coven kept a piece as a memento. The individual pieces represented individual incarnations but, when all tied together around our circle, were symbolic of the eternal nature of the deceased's spirit. We lit incense that rose high into the air, another symbolic gesture for assisting the departed to the land of the dead. We also filled and emptied a cauldron of water. In world mythology, water is closely linked to the land of the dead, and many of these Otherworld realms must be reached by crossing a river or sea. Water is also a symbol of the blood of the womb of the mother Goddess. The cauldron in Celtic mythology also represents that womb, the place from which we all start, end, and begin again the journey of life.

It was not unusual for us to be gifted with some sign that the spirit for whom we were doing the ritual was present. Our experiences are similar to those of other covens in that we could sense, smell, or feel the touch of the spirit. Sometimes we could see or hear the departed. Our detractors say this is because the group mind had willed itself a mass hallucination, but I believe that, as Witches, we are simply more open to the psychic phenomena that surround us. In other words, we don't have more psychic experiences than other people, we are just better able to recognize them.

Another rite of passage usually left solely in the hands of the coven is croning (as in the image of the crone Goddess) or elderhood (a term that can apply to both men and women), which is the celebration of the last third of life. In North American and European society we are taught to fight aging rather than honor it, and certainly never to embrace it as a positive life change. For women, the ritual may take place any time after menopause. For men, it usually occurs at some point in their fifties, when they feel that they have gained wisdom and entered the third stage of life.

Elderhood can be a confusing term for new Witches, who often read about someone quite young being an elder of their tradition. Elderhood is the achievement of age. Being an elder in a specific Craft tradition is reflective of knowledge, study, and the length of time spent within that tradition. In Clan Eireannach's tradition, one achieved the title of elder not by rushing through a study program but by having served nine years as a priest or priestess within our tradition. One becomes an elder at this point whether or not someone else is around to make a formal declaration.

Elderhood, or aging, rituals can also be done solitarily, but having younger people validate this experience, as is done in a coven setting, can be the psychological boost that takes the aging person from reciting mere words to truly knowing that she or he is special and valued just for being who and what he or she is.

In contrast to Western society as a whole, in the Craft we honor our elderly. Their opinions, experiences, and personal worth are valued and respected. These rituals of aging involve the acknowledgement of the wisdom, both secular and spiritual, that they have accrued over the course of their lives, and is an affirmation that there is still much more to look forward to.

One woman who celebrated her croning in Clan Eire-annach asked that we have as many mirrors in the circle as was safely possible. Older women are taught that the mirror is their enemy, that it merely points out all the wrinkles and laugh lines that should be despised, that it shows a face no one should love—including its owner. Biddy wanted to blast that idea to shards by making sure that everywhere she looked she could see a reflection of her face. In the ritual she proudly embraced her aging, and told us that each wrinkle was a badge of honor that she earned by surviving life's ups and downs. She even managed to brilliantly relate the derogatory term "crow's feet" to the crow, which is the totem animal of some of the Celtic crone Goddesses.

Like rituals of aging, Western cultures have fallen away from acknowledging the spiritual adulthood of their youth. Virtually all old Pagan cultures had a ceremony to mark this transition for both males and females, a custom that is kept alive in modern Witchcraft.

In the spring of 1989 one of our members, Liban, had a daughter who was ready for her coming of age ceremony. Liban had been a single mother for six years, and had raised her children in the Craft since her divorce. None of us doubted that the girl, Lisa, was ready to take her place among us as a spiritual adult. Liban was very anxious that we do all we could to remove the culturally imposed fear of menstruation from Lisa. Before the ritual, the women of the coven took Lisa out to dinner and gave her gifts to symbolize her womanhood, and told her stories about the positive aspects of being female. Then we escorted her to the circle, where she was honored with the white, red, and black initiation cord and allowed to choose her adult Craft name. We also had her bring along some of the blood from her first menses and placed it upon the altar where it was honored as a sacred object. Afterward, Lisa took charge of the ritual, her first time as acting leader.

Celebrating the Lunar Cycles

Clan Eireannach met monthly on the full moon, or as near to it as we could all meet. This is the most common meeting time for any coven, though some will chose to meet on the new moon instead, and a few energetic covens will meet at both times.

A monthly meeting timed by the lunar cycle is known as the esbat, from the Old French *esbattre* meaning "to frolic." At the esbat it is traditional to Draw Down the Moon, meaning that one member of the coven, usually the acting high priestess, takes the essence of the Goddess—as symbolized by the full moon—into herself. This is done by pulling the power of the moon into a ritual tool, then transferring it into a living body. If done right, it can be a very moving and powerful ceremony in which the Goddess speaks to the coven. If done wrong, or with wrong intent, it can be an excuse to lash out at the group, address petty jealousies, and drive away any hope of divinity coming into the circle.

In Clan Eireannach we never had to worry about anyone abusing the privilege of being the vessel of the Goddess, but I have been in groups where this has happened, and I have heard dreadful stories of such abuses in other groups. To be blunt, anyone who would stoop to using a sacred setting to press personal grievances is neither mature nor responsible enough to be part of a coven, and the rest of the group should have a long talk about what actions to take.

At the esbat, songs are sung in praise of the moon, the Cone of Power is raised, and any magick that is needed is performed. We finish the ritual with the Ceremony of Cakes and Ale. In this ceremony, a blessed grain product, such as cake or bread, and a blessed beverage, such as wine or fruit juice, are consecrated as the body and blood of the Goddess. Sometimes one or the other is assigned as being a representation of the God, and combining the two becomes a symbol of divine unity.

After esbat gatherings, Clan Eireannach would remain inside the circle enjoying one another's company, eating, and planning our next month's activities.

Celebrating the Solar Cycles

The solar festivals, known as the sabbats, have been written about time and time again. I also wrote an entire book on the subject. The festivals date back many thousands of years to western Europe, where our Pagan ancestors marked the changing of the seasons by the position of the sun. Some of these festivals have come down into modern times with surprisingly few changes. This is because the Christian Church, in its frenzy to stamp out Pagan ways, could not wholly eradicate the sabbats from the lives of the people. Instead they opted to graft a Christianized veneer onto the holidays. This is how Samhain became Halloween and why Christmas still uses so many Pagan symbols in its celebration (i.e.; decorated trees, wreaths, holly, and mistletoe).

The following are the sabbats of Witchcraft:

Samhain (October 31) is a festival that celebrates the end of summer, when the worlds of the living and the dead are open to one another. It also honors the dying of the old God and celebrates the Goddess as the powerful crone.

Yule (Winter Solstice) honors the rebirth of the God as symbolized by the newly waxing sun.

Imbolg/Oimelc (February 1 or 2) celebrates the awakening earth, the Goddess as the bride of the sun, and the lactation of ewes.

Ostara (Spring Equinox) is a fertility feast that honors the awakening sexuality of the young God and Goddess, and the rebirth of the earth after her winter's sleep.

Beltane/Bealtaine (May 1) is a fertility festival that honors the sacred marriage of the God and Goddess as symbolized by the weaving of the maypole.

Litha (Summer Solstice) celebrates the sun God (or Goddess) at his peak of power, and honors the earth Goddess who is pregnant with the coming harvest.

Lammas/Lughnasadh (August 1 or 2) celebrates the first harvest, the gathering of summer produce and grain. This is sometimes celebrated as the time of the corn king's (a God) death by self-sacrifice, or as the marriage of the Irish sun God Lugh with his queen.

Mabon (Autumn Equinox) honors the aging deities, marks the second harvest (berries and apples especially), and has been used as a time to pay honor to the dead at their final resting places.

The origin of the word *sabbat* is from the Greek *sabatu,* meaning "to rest." Therefore, Clan Eireannach worked no magick at the solar festivals, a custom to which I still adhere. This custom of not performing magick at the sabbats is followed in many covens, but many others feel free to weave magick at will. There is no inherently right or wrong choice.

Because Imbolg is sacred to the Irish Goddess Brighid, and she is one of the primary deities of the Wittan tradition, this was a special sabbat for us. On February Eve we would hold lavish ceremonial rituals in her honor, presided over by any in our group who were priests or priestesses of Brighid. The following day we carried her image into our circle as a bride, not just of the newly waxing sun, but of our own spirits as well.

Lughnasadh is sacred to the Irish God Lugh, the other primary deity of our tradition. We held similar ceremonial rituals in his honor that featured feasting and both marriage and death imagery.

Of all the sabbats, the one that most greatly intrigues those not in the Craft is Samhain, the festival from which our modern Halloween observance comes. There are many ways in which the festival is celebrated in covens, and Clan Eireannach's ritual had its unique elements as well as the universal themes.

Since the precise date of Samhain has been given in different sources as any time from October 28 through November 15, we chose to meet on October 30. This way we took advantage of the rising energies of anticipation, both from the Pagan and the secular world, and it left us free to enjoy Samhain parties or trick-or-treating the following night. Like many Wiccan traditions, we acknowledged that the lines of separation between the world of the living and the world of the dead are blurred on Samhain, and that we are each able to enter into the other's realm. We honored our beloved dead, bringing their photographs into our circle and calling out their names on our roll of remembrance. Each name was then torn from the list and tossed into an iron cauldron. Cauldrons are symbolic of the womb of the great mother Goddess from whom we are all born, and to whom we must return to await rebirth. When all the names were inside the cauldron we would burn them, symbolically setting the souls free. We mourned the death of the old God, and acknowledged the power of the crone Goddess who will rebirth him on the Winter Solstice, and whose promise of life renewed will see us through the dark days ahead.

We also observed the Dumb Supper, or Feast of the Dead. This is a meal at which places are set for the spirits. Living persons who sit down to the supper must eat in silence, hence the term "dumb." Any foods are appropriate offerings, but breads and cakes are traditional, as are red-colored drinks to symbolize the blood of life.

In Celtic traditions, Samhain marks the end of the old year and the beginning of the new. Unlike some Celtic traditions, Witta embraces rather than rejects its Norse influences, and because the Norse Pagan traditions celebrate the new year at the Winter Solstice, we usually had a spirited debate about just when the old year really ended. Though it is not Wittan tradition to do so, we acknowledged both dates—Samhain as a spiritual new year, and the Winter Solstice as a physical one.

Other Festivals and Resources

Depending on the culture from which a coven takes its practices, other lunar or solar festivals during the year may be observed. In Clan Eireannach, we adopted some other Irish festivals and honored the Caillach, or crone Goddess, on December 31, and celebrated the Puck Fair, honoring the horned God, in mid-August.

The lunar cycles, solar festivals, and rites of passage are central features of the Craft experience. Therefore, a wise Witch will learn as much about these subjects as she or he can. If you are lacking in this area, you will find below a brief listing of books that cover these subjects in whole or in part. Many of them contain ritual transcripts for you to use, or on which to model your own rituals.

Rites of Passage (St. Paul: Llewellyn, 1992); *Ancient Ways* (St. Paul: Llewellyn, 1992); and *The Wheel of the Year* (St. Paul: Llewellyn, 1994) by Pauline and Dan Campanelli.

The Grandmother of Time (San Francisco: Harper and Row, 1979) and *Grandmother Moon* (San Francisco: Harper and Row, 1991) by Zsuzsanna E. Budapest.

Celebrate the Earth (New York: Dell, 1994) by Laurie Cabot.

Witchcraft Today, Book II: Modern Rites of Passage (St. Paul: Llewellyn, 1993) edited by Chas S. Clifton.

Moon Magick (St. Paul: Llewellyn, 1995) by D. J. Conway.

Wicca: A Guide for the Solitary Practitioner (St. Paul: Llewellyn, 1988) by Scott Cunningham.

Eight Sabbats for Witches (Custer, WA: Phoenix, 1981) and *The Witches' Bible Complete* (Custer, WA: Phoenix, 1979) by Janet and Stewart Farrar.

The Sabbats (St. Paul: Llewellyn, 1993); *Lady of the Night* (St. Paul: Llewellyn, 1995); and *Entering the Summerland* (St. Paul: Llewellyn, 1996) by Edain McCoy.

The Turning of the Wheel (York Beach, ME: Weiser, 1994) by Stanley J. A. Modrzyk.

Seasons of the Sun (York Beach, ME: Weiser, 1996) by Patricia Telesco.

Chapter 9

INTER-COVEN NETWORKING and WITCH WARS

ONE OF THE ASPECTS I LIKED BEST about working with Clan Eireannach was the opportunity it afforded for networking with other covens. Through these channels I was able to meet lots of other Witches and Pagans. I was able to learn how they worshiped, what traditions they came from, and what they were searching for in their spiritual lives. We met occasionally with these other groups to celebrate life cycle events (see Chapter 8) and for festival gatherings that were sometimes open to all interested persons in the region.

Group networking is useful when you need to find out information about a specific tradition, culture, myth, et cetera, and have exhausted your research sources. Someone, somewhere in the Craft usually has the knowledge you're looking for or can tell you where to find it. Another use for networking arises when you have a student who is gifted in an area in which neither you nor anyone in your coven is skilled enough to teach. Someone else who does have the skill is usually happy to help.

Networking essentially means putting the word out to the community that your coven is there. Occasionally, non-Pagan folks hear about you. Sometimes this is good, because it creates interest and helps us disseminate accurate information about our religion. Sometimes it is bad, particularly when folks who are hostile to Paganism find their way to you.

For example, at one inter-coven gathering I attended, three young women attempted to challenge us. They were clearly afraid of us, and shaking so hard I thought they would pass out. We had registered at the state park where we were meeting and reserved covered picnic space under the name "South Texas Celtic Coven Network." The name was one we essentially picked out of the air, since no firm alliance existed other than our desire to get to know each other better. Later we had to assume that it was this registration that had fallen into the hands of the three women.

We first noticed them as they drove rapidly up the road in front of the picnic shelter, parked with a jolt, and raced out of the car, running headlong towards us as if it were pouring rain. Then, a few yards from the shelter, they stopped dead still, staring at us as if they were unsure of what to do next.

None of us spoke to the odd trio. I suppose we were all waiting to see what would happen. That was when my empathic senses registered that the women were afraid of us, and I was sure at this point that they were not Pagan. The bravest of the trio stepped forward and, with a trembling forearm, raised a cross as if warding off vampires. Yes, I kid you not. It was a heavy silver cross that looked as if it had recently been lifted from some church's chancel. I know most of us were smirking by this time. How could we help it? The sight was so silly.

The brave one found her voice and spouted some Biblical nonsense I cannot remember. I think it may have been something about repentance and turning from evil, or perhaps it was the "not suffer a Witch to live" passage which, thanks to King James' deliberate mistranslation, equated Witches with poisoners. From behind me I heard a man say, "Blessed be, sisters, the Goddess welcomes you."

Many of our group had to turn away to avoid laughing right in the women's faces. The invitation sounded so tongue-in-cheek, yet if the trio had actually wanted to sit with us and exchange intelligent ideas, they would have been welcome.

The bug-eyed threesome remained silent. I am not sure what they expected, but I am positive that it was not words of welcome. They were armed for battle, and I think they were disappointed that we were not accommodating. After a moment of silence they came to life at once, each quoting different Bible verses and sounding like a re-enactment of the Tower of Babel myth, since none of their utterings made any sense in relation to the events that were unfolding. I held my breath, hoping that the Witchy folks I was with had enough sense not to try and engage the women in verbal battle. They were not there to learn, but to challenge, and nothing we said was going to do anything but further convince them of their righteousness.

The man who had spoken to them before stepped to the front of the shelter, and I winced, sure that he was going to lose his cool and start a war. Instead, the man offered them welcome again, and asked if they wished to join us.

Wrong move! The ladies immediately took this as an invitation from one of Satan's own to join up, and they retreated a few steps. Without offering any further explanation, the man stood aside and, motioning to the nearest picnic table, said, "You're welcome to share our feast."

Before the women could come up with an appropriate retort, one of them noticed another picnic table at the edge of the shelter that was set up as a communal altar. We intended to use it as the focus of a group ritual later in the evening, but for the time being it was sitting out in plain sight, adorned with sacred objects, tools, stones, unlit candles, and statuary. The woman who noticed it pointed and screamed, a high-pitched aural assault that made my ears ache. She babbled something unintelligible that the other two apparently understood. As soon as their eyes locked onto the altar they all squealed like a chorus of banshees, and fled as if (pardon the pun) they were being chased by the very devil.

We all actually found the event amusing, mostly because of the abject fear involved. We also knew that this situation could have been much worse, even dangerous for us, if the women had gone to gather new recruits for a second assault. As much as we wanted to open ourselves to the Craft community, we exercised more caution in the future in how we booked park reservations.

Clan Eireannach most enjoyed meeting with other covens for some of the major sabbats (see Chapter 8).

Usually we selected two or three of our number to work with representatives from the other covens to create a ritual with which all would be comfortable. The need to be flexible is essential in this type of networking. The point is not just to work together, but to learn from each other, try new ideas, and forge new links with the divine. After the ritual format and content are set, scripts are copied and distributed among all the coven members so that everyone can memorize their parts and know what to expect.

One of the best networking events of this type was held at that same state park where the three fundy women accosted us. This time we did not register ourselves at the campground under any name that would be suspect. We spent the weekend before Samhain at the campground together, sharing and eating. I don't know what it is when magickal folks get together, but everyone always seems to have copious amounts of food on hand!

We had obtained permission to hold a full-blown religious ritual in the park. I think the park officials wanted to deny us permission, but they often allowed Christian groups to worship there and could not legally deny us the same right. We told them we intended to keep the event quiet, and that we wanted to do this after sunset back off one of the hiking trails where there was not likely to be any traffic. To ease their minds all the more, we gave them a copy of the ritual script and told them they were welcome to join us. This immediately allayed their suspicions that we might be doing something heinous, like sacrificing animals.

After sundown all five of our covens, totalling about forty people, began the trek back along the hiking trail. What you have to remember is that nearly all of us were city people, urbanites whose hiking expertise had been gained largely through mowing the lawn on weekends. Put three dozen city Witches in the woods at night and you've got a proverbial three-ring circus on your hands. Even with flashlights someone was tripping over something every few minutes, and a few members of the group were terrified of getting lost. Others worried about running into less-than-pleasant critters, always a real danger in Texas, but we reasoned that even the fiercest javelina or largest rattler would flee when our clumsy feet came stomping around. One woman's odd sense of humor moved her to lead us in a chorus of the "Heigh Ho" song from Disney's *Snow White and the Seven Dwarves* as we marched along.

We finally made it to our ritual site with no more casualties than a few skinned knees and began lighting our working candles (all globed for outdoor safety, of course) at what would be the perimeter of our circle. The area we chose was a good-sized clearing created by a rocky formation that protruded above the ground. In daylight, it offered a panoramic view of the river below, and on a starry night seemed poised on the edge of the universe.

As the ritual took shape in the silence of the night woods we could feel, and in some cases actually see, the presence of the spirit world hovering at the edge of our sacred space. At one point Liban elbowed me and pointed up at the tree branches looming over the clearing, and I gasped in awe. There were the dryads, the tree spirits, smiling mischievously down at us, their own special music faintly filing the air.

When the ritual came to an end, no one was ready to leave the enchanted environment we had created. We all sat down on the rocky ground around the edge of the circle. We sang, talked, shared spells, told spirit stories, did guided meditations, and forged a bond with nature and the Otherworld that I have never felt so strongly since.

Time is irrelevant inside the circle, and it is customary not to bring watches or other time pieces inside, so we had no idea what hour it was when we finally decided it was time to close the circle and head back for the campground. It seemed a shame to banish the mysterious and potent energies that were still awash in the air around us. When we finally did close the circle and make our way back to camp, we were stunned to discover it was after three in the morning. We had been in the circle for nearly seven hours!

Before leaving the park the next afternoon, we made sure that our camp area was completely clean. This is not only a courtesy to other park visitors, but shows respect for Mother Earth, and leaves a good impression of Witches on those who operate the campground. Always, always, leave any outdoor camp or ritual site in better shape than you found it.

The Down Side of Inter-Coven Connections

When covens get to know each other, members become privy to the internal ups and downs each group struggles with on a month-to-month basis. If a coven's energy is positive, you can learn a lot from them about working out your own coven's upheavals. If a coven has taken a negative turn, which happens easily when internal problems are left to fester like an open wound, you will find the warring factions trying to suck you into the battle and forcing you to choose sides.

Such battles divide a community that should be presenting a united front, if for no other reason than mutual support in a world that still hears the word "Witch" and wants to start gathering kindling. When these conflicts cannot be solved, a coven will often split into two warring groups. Unfortunately, the aftermath of these explosive break-ups can have a lasting and detrimental impact on the local Pagan community as the combatants wage their "Witch war." This is a term heard all too often in Craft circles, and refers to problems that are not allowed to pass, but instead escalate to encompass a sizable number of individuals and covens.

All the covens Clan Eireannach met with on a regular basis seemed to be thriving, or at least holding their own. I do not recall any serious internal squabbles or divisions that threatened to split or destroy any of the covens we knew personally, nor do I recall gossip and backstabbing being a particular problem. However, once these channels of contact are open and the grapevine linking your coven to others takes root, all sorts of interesting tales and intrigues present themselves.

I recall hearing about one Witch war in Texas that got to be dubbed "The Great Chicken Bone War." Neither I nor anyone in Clan Eireannach or in our network actually knew the combatants, but I believe that nearly every Witch in the state was aware of the event before the furor it caused died down. I cannot attest to the exact chain of events that led to the war. I can only relate what I heard from sources who claimed to have first-hand information.

A large coven somewhere in the Austin area apparently divided into two smaller covens over an issue surrounding leadership. The group that left the main body was allowed to go peacefully, but somehow they did not think that this was the case and were ever on guard for signs of psychic attack. One day one of the leaders of the splinter group found chicken bones in his garbage and decided they were placed there to curse him and those who left the original coven. In the Brujeria tradition, a negative path with Mexican roots that has a following in south Texas, chicken bones are often used in negative magick.

The parent coven disavowed any knowledge of the bones, claiming, sensibly enough, that the garbage is where old bones belong, and that the leader of the new coven was crazy. This led both sides into a magickal war. Curses and lightning bolts were lobbed through the cosmos with the aim of blasting each other to ashes. The worst part was that the community at large, non-Craft people, picked up on the story. It was very embarrassing.

I never heard any more about the combating covens after this, but it would be safe to assume that they both sunk in a mire of their own making and no longer exist.

In spite of Witch wars, you will find that most of your experiences networking with other groups will be positive. Mine certainly have been. I only relate the less-than-pleasant stories because you need to be aware that there are less-than-pleasant people out there, and because they make interesting anecdotes in Craft circles.

If you do find yourself in a bad situation, walk away. Chances are if you are uncomfortable, someone else is too, and you may have company when you go. Just keep in mind that walking away means letting go. Put the problem from your mind and avoid hurling negative words or magick back at the coven. No community needs another Great Chicken Bone War.

Chapter 10

TEACHING SECRETS

and

SECRET TEACHINGS

NOT ALL COVENS ARE TEACHING COVENS. I have been involved in both, and prefer helping newcomers find a way in. I can't help but remember how grateful I was to have someone help me when I was starting out. Being part of a teaching coven has its own special rewards and frustrations, but then the same could probably be said by any teacher of any subject. As I have already mentioned, Clan Eireannach maintained an outer circle of students, many of whom formed their own covens and began to teach others when their study with us was complete. The students sometimes worked with us in our circle, and at other times met separately, often with one of us in attendance to give guidance.

Today, teaching the Craft is much easier than it used to be. Paganism in the 1990s is more public than it has been for centuries, with books, courses, and periodicals available in abundance to provide in-depth resources for private study. Most students who come to today's covens for teaching already have a strong background, and are merely looking for instruction within a specific tradition, rather than needing the basics.

After fifteen years in the Craft I have come to the conclusion that the Witches with the most well-rounded educations are the ones that have learned from a combination of books and personal teachers.

A variety of books will provide different points of view for students to consider. You don't have to agree with, or even like, everything in any single book, but you should be willing to understand the point of view expressed and accept it as a valid expression of the Craft. I still read most of the Craft books for beginners that come out, and I find there is something to be learned from each one.

Having at least one personal teacher in your life will initiate you into the mysteries for which there are no sufficient words of description. Every Pagan contact you meet is a potential teacher, no matter how long you have been in the Craft. There is always something new to learn.

How Clan Eireannach Organized Its Teaching Circle

Knowing that a student would make contact with one of us when she or he was ready, and that he or she would request initiation either in Witta or basic Wicca, we formulated a written plan that would best suit our teaching style and the needs of each type of applicant. This plan became an amendment to our coven compact.

1. The contacted coven member will make an assessment of the knowledge the student already possesses. In some cases this may be considerable, with the student having already been initiated into another tradition or having undergone self-dedication after several years of private study. The contacted member must also get the student's proof of age. For legal reasons, we cannot instruct minors.

2. If the contacted member feels that the student is right for our outer circle, she or he must arrange for several private meetings to talk with and get to know the applicant on a personal level. If the contacted member still feels the student is right, he or she should make arrangements for the student to meet with the entire inner circle.

3. If the coven feels that the student will fit into the outer circle, arrangements must be made for the student to meet with the other students. As they essentially form a coven of their own, even if their association is only temporary, their permission for the newcomer to join them must be secured.

4. If permission is granted, the student will be paired with a primary teacher from the inner circle, based on who has an opening for a

student and on personal feelings of compatibility between student and teacher.

5. The teacher and student will set a time frame for completion of studies and will schedule their own meetings. The teacher will be responsible for making arrangements with other members of the coven to teach in areas in which she or he lacks expertise.

6. The student will be expected to make every effort to meet with the teacher and coven when scheduled. The student must also decide what type of initiation, if any, is desired at the end of training. This information must be passed along to the teacher, who will enter it into the coven's teaching records.

7. The student is free to contact any other members of the coven to ask questions, get special assistance, or address any grievances against the primary teacher. The student may also request a new primary teacher if he or she feels the relationship is not working. However, if the reason for the desired change is found to be lack of effort to complete assigned lessons, the request will be denied.

8. At the end of the study period, the student will undergo an examination conducted by the entire inner circle to ensure that sufficient knowledge and skill has been acquired.

The next step was to update our teaching chart, a necessary bit of paperwork to ensure that the training of each student was being carried out in accordance with the student's wishes and needs, so that nothing the student needed was overlooked by us. A typical teaching chart is shown on the two following pages.

Charting out this information helped keep us on track. No one's initiation got overlooked, no one's talents were wasted, and it helped us to give the students our best attention. For example, Liban was an impressive healer. Niamh's student, who was interested and gifted in this art, was sent to study healing with Liban. I, in turn, took Liban's student, who wanted to improve his astral projection techniques—an area in which I excel.

After the required lessons were learned, and the proper amount of time had passed, formal initiation would be made if the student so wished.

Other Teaching Coven Structures

Clan Eireannach's organization worked for us and, I believe, for our students as well, but there are numerous ways to organize a teaching coven besides the inner and outer circle method.

Some covens have the teacher bring the student to every coven function. Students worship with their teachers in the same circles, stand next to them during rituals, assist them in coven magick, and in general learn side by side as the teacher participates in the regular activities of the coven. Covens of this type are usually quite large, with the student becoming part of the group after initiation. This was the structure of the first coven of which I was a part. I believe it had sixty-plus members, none of whom made it to every gathering.

Clan Eireannach's Teaching Chart — Last Update, November 16

Teacher	Student	Date Began	Expected End Date	Notes
DeDannan, Eriu (Roo)	Jeff/Lugh	9-15	2-1	Extensive Craft background. Initiated as a Gardnerian in 1984. Wants a Wittan initiation. Hopes to join coven forming from outer circle.
O'Sean, Macha	Lisa/Nemetona	N/A	12-16	Liban's daughter. Raised in Craft for last six years. Wants combination Coming of Age and initiation ritual. Hopes to form a teen coven, either Eclectic or Wittan.
McCoy, Edain	Lianna/Grainne	6-19	6-20	New Craft student. Wants initiation as Eclectic. Appears skilled in various forms of divination. Interested in dreams.
O'Neill, Bran	Ryan/Tuan	7-6	11-1	Has been a solitary for three years. Self-taught and displays sound Craft knowledge. Wants to be part of Wittan tradition, and asks that we accept his self-initiation.
McDairmuid, Dana	N/A			

Name				Notes
O'Connell, Liban	Cory/Merlin	4-3	10-30	Was initiated into an English traditional coven and asks us to accept this. He is looking to improve certain skills such as astral projection and past life work.
McBride, Niamh	Sarah/Flidais	8-31	1-1	Gifted with animals. Shows talent as a healer. Has studied on her own for two years. Wants to learn Eclectic Wicca and be initiated into Witta. Hopes to join outer-circle coven.
Windwalker, Taranus (Tari)	N/A			
MacRoi, Sionnan	N/A			
Oakgrove, Holly	(Currently assessing a potential student)			
NiArmagh, Biddy	Candy/Airmid	5-5	5-6	Craft newcomer. Wants to learn Eclectic Wicca. Seems to have an affinity for magickal herbalism. Has made no decisions about a coven or specific tradition she wants to follow, but she does want an initiation.
MacRuadh, Finn	Jennifer/Fand	3-31	4-1	Relatively new to Craft, but has done lots of reading and experimenting. Interested in all Celtic paths. Wants to be initiated as a Witch and Wittan, and would like to join the outer-circle coven. Displays bardic talents.

Other covens set up a rotation system so that the student has many different teachers, perhaps one each month or each season. There may or may not be an inner circle involved, but students get to know everyone in the coven fairly well. The advantage to this set-up is that the student experiences a variety of teachings and ideas. The drawback is that it lacks opportunity for the close bonding that might otherwise occur between student and teacher.

Some covens teach the students all at once, usually at rituals and other planned gatherings. Open discussions, question and answer periods, and book reviews are usually part of the curriculum.

The Teaching Experience

Most of the students who came to Clan Eireannach wanted to be a part of the Wittan tradition, and already had a fair to excellent background in Witchcraft. These students were serious, excelled at their studies, and became valued members of our network. A few others were new to the Craft, and wanted to learn basic Wicca. The majority of these were sincere in their efforts to learn and, whether they stayed with us or moved on, someone out there is lucky to be working with them today.

Then there were the others…. Every classroom has its problem children, right? Well, so it is in Witchcraft.

As any of you who have been in the Craft for a long time know, you learn to sort out pretty quickly who will be receptive to learning and who merely wants to beat drums, chant, and toss around a little magick. Members of this second group are usually the ones who are attracted to the label "Witch." They love the mysterious sound, they love shocking others, and mostly they love accruing personal power. They are not really interested in spirituality and are antagonistic to authority of any kind. Because they perceive you in an authoritarian role, they become antagonistic to your teachings. Often they can fool you at first. These types pretend to go along in the beginning, then after a few months decide they know more than you do, and break away to do Goddess knows what.

Learning the Craft is *work*. It takes effort and an ego that is willing to admit that the mind it is attached to does not know everything there is to know. Many Craft students drop out before their initiation because they simply do not want to work—for anything.

I met one such individual at an open study circle. My friend, Inanna, was developing the circle into a teaching organization. This young man had read three whole Craft books (yes, so many!) and had only been involved in study for about two months. At the end of this time, he told her that he hadn't learned a thing from her, that she wasn't a real Witch because she wouldn't go skyclad, and that she was an elitist for having an inner circle to which the students were not privy. He also told her that he didn't need her hierarchy (this was a strictly egalitarian group!), and that he thought he would join the Gardnerians.

Inanna had trouble not laughing at him. The Gardnerian tradition has a strict hierarchy based on earned degrees, and specific initiation rites given at each stage. Their initiatory tradition also requires that you be initiated by one of their members who has attained a certain degree in order to even be considered a Gardnerian Witch. After he left, I heard he made a few attempts to start his own coven, but I have no idea whether or not he managed to dupe newcomers into viewing him as a Gardnerian high priest.

I once had a student, a young man named David, who started off with a lot of promise. He was relatively new to the Craft, but had been doing a lot of self-study over the previous year. I am always thrilled when students question my ideas, my sources, and my theology. This is how they learn and develop their own unique perspective on Witchcraft. Over the course of a few months I began to notice that David's questions had taken on a hostile tone, and he seemed to resent each new month's study assignments. Finally he came to me and said that Clan Eireannach expected too much of him, and that he didn't need all this formality just to become Pagan. He announced that he was going to go out and find some nice Druids to study with.

Like Inanna, I found it hard to contain my mirth. In the old days, Druids studied intensely for twenty years to obtain the right to their initiation and status in the Celtic community. Modern Druidism does not quite take a lifetime to master, but most orders do have a rigorous set of guidelines and program of study. Getting into a Druidic order usually takes longer than the traditional year and a day required by most Wiccan/Pagan covens. New Druids are very well-educated by the time they complete their studies. While I do not always agree with Druidic viewpoints, I have never met a Druid whose magickal and mythological knowledge I did not respect. I have no idea what happened to David, but I'd be willing to bet that, to his mind, the Druids expected too much of him, too.

On the plus side of teaching, it is a real joy to watch someone you've helped excel and grow and become a fine Craft leader. You have the satisfaction of knowing that this is a balanced individual who is a credit to the Pagan community. If it was the right situation for student and teacher, both of you will come away from the encounter more knowledgeable than you were before.

Those You Should Probably Not Teach

Aside from those people you assess to be not really interested, power hungry, or (do I dare say it?) just plain crazy, it is wise to steer away from two groups: minors and close friends.

It is sad that minors are generally being excluded from covens. The only ones Clan Eireannach taught were the children of our inner-circle members. There have been too many cases of parents threatening to sue covens and individual Craft teachers for giving instruction without parental permission. Even though freedom of religion is an on-paper right in most Western societies, we all know that, for minors and for those following off-the-beaten-path traditions, the same rights under the law do not always apply. Parents have a right to instruct minors in the religion of their choice, or to avoid spiritual teaching altogether. However, I feel it is sad when children today express an interest in anything spiritual, but are discouraged because the faith in which they are interested does not conform to their parents' expectations.

I have read about covens that have attempted to get around the legal problems by meeting with the parents themselves to allay their fears. They also have the young students produce a notarized letter of permission from a parent. The drawback here is that even if one parent agrees, another might still be outraged, especially if the parents are not living together and do not get along. The other parent may still try to sue you.

I have heard more than a few miserable tales about friends teaching friends, after which they were friends no longer. Whether we like it or not, a teacher and a student are in an unequal relationship. Even though both may be learning from the experience, be the same age, be from the same background, have become friendly, et cetera, a teacher is still in a position of "advantage" over the student. When it comes to teaching persons with whom you are friends, these factors put you at risk of losing the friendship.

Think about it. How easy would it be for you to set lessons down in front of your friend and expect him or her to do them, then grade them and tell your friend what he or she did wrong? These actions defy the definition of friendship as a partnership of equals.

About a year ago a good friend of mine, Zorya, became interested in Wicca and, after a bumpy start, asked me to teach her. I had been somewhat afraid she would approach me with this request. I wanted her to get the teaching she so badly wanted, but I also knew what havoc the arrangement could wreak on our relationship. I explained to her my reservations, and although she listened, she kept insisting that she thought the year and day of study would strengthen, not weaken, our friendship.

I took her on, and I must admit that the road has not has as many potholes as I anticipated. I also know that I have been less demanding of her than I should have been, and have occasionally asked for help from another Wiccan we both know. I believe that Zorya and I have been lucky, and I only hope that her training is as complete as it should be as she approaches her initiation this November. If asked to teach a friend again, I would politely decline.

It is good to keep in mind that you are not obligated to teach anyone. Some Witches prefer not to teach simply because they do not feel talented in this area. There is an old legend that says that no Witch can die until he or she passes along his/her knowledge to a younger Witch. Who knows, perhaps withholding wisdom has its merits as well!

The Veiled Workings of the Inner Circle

Nearly all covens have some type of secret rituals that it swears all members keep and protect. This is one of those "Witch things" that is commonly known outside of Pagan circles, and has led outsiders to believe that this is how we guard the machinations of our evil practices.

Traditionally, secrets have been kept:

1. As a necessary precaution in the days of the Witch hunters to protect the coven and its members from death. Since then it has simply become a custom.

2. To protect rituals from being copied and practiced by those who do not know how to handle the energy being raised. During the centuries of Witch persecutions, false

information was purposely handed out when Witches were caught and tortured so that the true workings of the coven would be carried into the silence of the grave.

3. To guard the efficacy of ritual and magickal workings by not dividing the energy among those who would not contribute to the outcome, or who would actively work to undermine the coven's efforts.

Usually the elements that are held secret involve:

1. The identities of coven members and the location of the covenstead, both carry-overs from the Witch-hunting days, when lives depended on these secrets.

2. Methods of invoking deity, names of deities, and the names and manner of calling on other spirits or elementals who regularly assist the coven.

3. Special rituals that have been devised by the tradition or coven that they wish to keep to themselves to enhance the power and efficacy of their workings.

In modern life, promises are easily broken, and some modern Witches admit to not worrying about perishing should death oaths be taken and later discarded. Whether they have anything concrete to worry about remains to be seen, but in either case we have to put this custom in its historical perspective to understand it. Among some pre-Christian societies in Europe, one's word was sacred to an extent we can barely grasp today.

Once a vow was made, all the tortures and threats of an enemy could not have induced someone to break his/her word. In magickal circles one often hears the term "words of power." Words carry magickal intent, and uttering them, particularly in the name of a deity or of one's clan, binds the promise up in sacred magick.

Many Witches argue today that the age of secrets is past, and that it is time for the old mysteries to be shared with all. Indeed, many of the mysteries have been made public over the past decade. Sadly, portions of them have been misunderstood by students who have no teachers to fully explain the more esoteric concepts. No matter how strongly we think we view magickal powers, it is hard to be a modern person and not occasionally feel just a hint of disbelief that a magickal mistake could actually be dangerous, but it can. It is a generally accepted metaphysical belief that like energies attract like, and so it is difficult for a Witch to raise much more energy than she or he can handle, but occasionally surprises do occur. A friend and I almost learned the hard way when we attempted a scrying experiment without adequate protection and dredged up something unpleasant. Because of this experience, I have always felt that it is more sensible to hold on to certain coven teachings until you know the person to whom you are giving them is ready for the challenge. Other information can, and should, be made public so that we can all learn and grow.

In Clan Eireannach, we recognized within ourselves this ambivalence about keeping secrets. We felt that as much as possible about our practices should be made public, but we also felt the need to protect the integrity of the group, look after our students' well-being, and guard the efforts that went into our discoveries and magick. Instead of making death oaths about keeping permanent secrets, we took a nine-year vow to hold certain aspects of our practices in secret, many of which involved our own creations of Irish ritual magick. We agreed that if we were still together in nine years, we could decide then whether to renew those oaths of secrecy. If not, we would be free to pass along this information as we saw fit. As of September 1995 the nine years were over and, as our coven is no longer together, we are free to pass these teachings along under the guidance of our "harm none" edict.

Like the secrets of many covens, our work was based on well-known concepts and practices. Only the precise way in which we used this knowledge was our own. The rituals involved the invocation of numerous deities into the bodies of our coven members (see my earlier work, *Celtic Myth & Magick*, for a detailed discussion of this process), and then working involved ritual dramas in this state. The energies within the circle were fascinating, and we quickly found out which deities were not compatible with one another, and which combinations produced the best magickal energies.

If you join or form a coven that takes vows of secrecy, please make sure you have a good idea of why you are doing this. Don't do it just because it sounds fun and mysterious. Do it for reasons that will enhance your efforts, not your egos, and that will protect and guide newcomers, not leave them wondering what is going on.

Chapter 11

RESOLVING CONFLICTS
and
PARTING WAYS

BECAUSE THERE IS NO GOVERNING BODY standing in authority over Witchcraft, covens are on their own to resolve internal disputes. Sometimes conflicts can be worked out to everyone's satisfaction, but sometimes they cannot, and the coven members part ways.

Covens can be considered senior citizens if they are more than five years old. Some old-timers in the Craft will no doubt read this and argue, able to point to some shining examples of groups that have remained intact for a decade or more. My reply to them is that the very fact that these covens jump readily to mind shows that they are the exception, not the rule. In my experience, most covens that survive for the long term are either open in nature, and therefore have a lot of different faces passing in and out over the years, or else have at their core less than a half-dozen committed and skilled leaders who keep things going no matter what.

What kills covens? Surprisingly, few seem to break up over theological differences. Most of us who go into covens are ready to reconcile ourselves to some type of group mind, willing to compromise certain practices and ideas for the good of the group. Unfortunately, the differences that cause members to pack up and leave in anger usually involve either the coven structure itself or personal clashes with other members of the group. The two problems are often related and can most often be traced to petty jealousies.

Creative Problem Solving

Whatever upheavals befall your coven, taking steps to rectify the problem or, if this cannot be done, making an effort to part amicably is important not only to the spiritual well-being of everyone involved, but to the Craft community as well. Having a coven split into two warring factions is miserable for anyone within spell-shot. Recall my story of the Great Chicken Bone War from Chapter 9 if you need to be reminded just how ugly these break-ups can be.

Sometimes an individual within a coven transgresses the rules that the group has established. In these cases it should be a simple matter to fall back on the coven compact to decide how to deal with the problem. With a little open dialogue, a simple problem can usually be worked out to everyone's satisfaction. Even if it cannot, keeping a cool head will enable you to part ways in peace and love.

If you are a member of a coven and discover or sense that something between members is amiss, discuss your feelings with another coven member. This doesn't mean sit down and have a trashing gossip session. It means find out if anyone else feels as you do. If so, then it is time to sit the entire group down for a long talk.

Open dialogue should be moderated by an objective party if possible. Another Witch who is outside of your coven and has no personal stake in the outcome of the conflict is the best choice. This is where your networking pays off. If you cannot find another Witch, try contacting a Pagan organization in your area. Someone there might be willing to arbitrate for you. Remember that these people have no voice of authority within your coven, and they probably do not want one. They are present only to clarify points when things get confusing, to help each faction see the other's point of view, and to keep battles from breaking out.

When no moderator is available, I have known covens to employ the Native American idea of the "talking stick." This is a ritual staff or some other object which, when in someone's possession, allows that person to speak freely and without interruption until the object is passed on to the next person. This procedure serves two excellent functions. First, it allows each individual a chance to explain oneself without having to be interrupted with unproductive counter-arguments and, second, it allows people to rethink angry or hurtful words while they are waiting for the stick to be passed to them.

If your coven is part of a hierarchical tradition, you may have elders in your group whose job it is to moderate disputes, mete out punishments, or hand down decisions.

Depending on how the tradition is organized, their word may or may not be binding upon the coven. If you do not like this, you are free to leave and find a tradition that operates differently. Remember that you chose this tradition in the first place—no one forced you—and you owe the coven the respect of leaving peaceably if you do not wish to abide by the judgments of its elders.

Consensus can also solve many problems. Consensus means coming to an agreement through dialogue; it also means compromise. For instance, if the problem under discussion involves a point of ritual, and you cannot come to a consentual agreement, allow the dissenters to have their way once in a while. Anyone so rigidly bound by ritual format that they cannot compromise occasionally probably should rethink being in a coven in the first place. Making temporary positive changes will not harm anyone, and it may ultimately save your group.

Sometimes a person's former religious background interferes in his/her relationship with a coven, whether he or she realizes it or not. Some Pagans who came from staunchly fundamentalist backgrounds grew up with this type of internal combat constantly taking place in their churches. When faced with uncertainty, people tend to fall back into old patterns if they don't make a conscious effort to overcome them. Even though this person may have made the leap to Paganism, the idea that there are many paths to deity may not yet have fully penetrated his/her consciousness. Pointing out these carryovers might help ease the tensions.

Sadly, disputes within covens often revolve around personalities, and these clashes are usually not resolvable in the long run. When two strong-willed people butt heads, even if their reasons are justified, the resentment they feel will only be magnified by the ritual circle, and the result is destructive.

When a coven becomes aware of such a situation between two people, tough decisions have to be made. To ask one party to leave the coven seems unfair and may anger that person's friends who remain within the group. To ask both to leave may be more fair, but does not usually leave those behind with the feeling that everything turned out well. I knew of one coven that put its two combatants inside a bedroom together for over an hour and told them to work out their problems or else. This tactic might have succeeded if the two people involved actually wanted to work things out. Instead, they used the time to finally say to each other all the ugly things they had held inside for so long. The air was fairly purple with their rage. In the end the coven broke up because nothing was resolved and, as the hostilities escalated, others were forced to take sides.

My way of dealing with two combatants is to tell them both that they must get along, and if any negativity from either of them is sensed inside the circle they will both have to go, regardless of who is causing the discord. If they really enjoy the company of the other coven members they will usually make an effort, but it is rarely a final solution. My next step is to ask the newest member to consider leaving the group, since the coven presumably got along fine before this person showed up. A woman in a discussion circle I once ran left after I told her, as kindly as I knew how, that she was upsetting a lot of people. I didn't realize just how insidious her influence was until a few weeks later, when one of the other women came to me and asked if I hadn't noticed that no one was mad at each other any more and there hadn't been a problem with gossip since Carmen left us. She was right. We later found Carmen had found her way into the negative path of Brujeria.

Unfortunately, sometimes it is not a single individual, or even two people, who are not happy with something that is happening. Sometimes it is an entire faction made up of members who have been discussing their dissatisfaction among themselves for quite a while. Instead of talking it out with the rest of the coven as they should have done in the first place, they allow their feelings of frustration to fester into anger and resentment. These situations usually cannot be patched up. The only course of action is splitting the coven into two smaller groups.

Such a split does not have to be a negative occurrence if all parties involved can keep the objective in mind, and avoid name-calling and hip-shot accusations. If you remain part of the original coven, do not fall into the trap of taking the desertion of these members personally. Remember that they have to follow their hearts, for better or worse. If you are part of the splinter group, avoid thinking that those you left behind are in the wrong. There are very few rights and wrongs in the Craft.

In some cases it will be the leadership of the coven itself that is called into question. Sometimes the motive behind this is power hunger or jealousy. At other times there may be a legitimate problem. In the latter case, don't count on the leader to quietly step down. When the leadership of a group deteriorates to the point that it cannot be fixed, it is time to move on, either alone or with others who share your dissatisfaction. Do this as peaceably as possible, without casting blame or hurling hurtful words and magick. You joined the coven of your own free will, and you may leave it the same way. Always know that it is never too late to pull out of a group if you are unhappy or are upset by things the group does. If the group is involved in what you deem to be dangerous or degrading practices, you should turn tail, run, and never look back.

If the one questioning the leadership of the group appears to be motivated from jealousy, it is time to sit down for one of those long sessions with the talking stick. Forcing the one making the accusations to put his/her concerns into clear, precise words can illuminate the root of the problem and make it clear to all whether the accusations have merit or not. If jealousy is the motive, the instigator will end up making him/herself look foolish and be forced to apologize or leave. Either way, the issue is at an end for your coven.

Banishing—An Act of Last Resort

Sometimes a transgression against the coven or its members is serious and unforgivable. When this happens the only course of action open to the coven may be banishment.

Banishment is a serious affair, an act of last resort when all other avenues of arbitration are closed. When you banish someone you remove them from your coven forever. Their ties with the group mind are ritually severed and their name is stricken from coven records, not to be uttered in sacred places again.

Sometimes covens will try to publish the fact that they have banished someone. Often this is done because the person has been found to be dangerous or unstable, and making the situation public is a way of warning other covens and solitaries about the person. At other times, however, it is a petty act designed only to belittle or disgrace someone who may or may not have committed any grievous sin. When you hear or read a notice of banishment keep the person's name in mind just in case, but unless you have firsthand knowledge of the situation, reserve judgment.

Banishment is a momentous undertaking, one that can rock the foundation of your coven and community, even when all agree that the action is for the best. Therefore, only the most serious offenses should be punished this way. These include:

- Situations in which a coven member has behaved in a way that has threatened to destroy the coven. For instance, she or he has spread gossip with malicious intent, or broken the vows of secrecy to the point that the workings of the group have been compromised.

- Situations in which a coven member has attempted to use the energy raised by the group for negative purposes without the knowledge or consent of the coven.

- Situations in which a coven member has directly taken actions to neutralize a magickal effort on which the entire coven worked.

- Situations in which a coven member has behaved in a manner that put one or more members of the coven in jeopardy. This could be any situation in which lives, health, or property have been put at significant risk.

- Situations in which trust has been breached. For example, the offender placed unrevealed substances in food intended for group consumption. This could be a drug, or even legal herbs that are known to have specific and unwanted effects on the body or psyche. The story in Chapter 6 about BadWitch bringing his pet tarantula into the circle is another example of broken trust.

- Situations in which sacred space or objects are defiled. This includes any action in which the sacred space is not honored as safe space, or makes it unfit as a dwelling place of the divine. Offenses in this category include treating ritual objects with contempt, showing disrespect for the deities, or purposefully disrupting rituals just for the pleasure of doing so.

There are probably as many rites of banishment as there are covens, but all include one objective: to sever the ties that the person has forged with the group mind of the coven so that his or her negative influence is removed from future efforts. I read about one coven that uses a blackthorn staff to sever these ties. Blackthorn is a wood used to level curses in many English traditions. I know of another coven that would create a poppet, or straw doll, in the image of the offender, then burn it in the ritual fire.

I do not advocate cursing anyone for any reason. Banishments can be done without sending unnecessary negativity to the offenders. Their own actions will eventually backfire and the Threefold Law take over. No need to add more.

Clan Eireannach never had to banish anyone (thank Goddess!), but the small coven in which BadWitch and I were members did. The ritual we created for this purpose was crafted with the input of everyone. We did not curse BadWitch, but we severed his emotional and psychic ties to us, as individuals and as a coven.

To begin, we cast our circle counter-clockwise, the direction associated with banishing. We called the quarters counter-clockwise also, explaining to them our purpose as each was evoked. At the center of the circle was a cast-iron cauldron partially filled with water, and on our altar sat eight white candles, as yet unlit. We also had on hand three-foot lengths of black yarn, one for each person present.

As priestess, I announced that we were gathered to banish BadWitch, to remove his presence from the energy cycle of our circle. We cut his name from our Book of Shadows and placed it into a paper boat folded by one of our members. Dousing the boat in lighter fluid, we placed it inside the cauldron and let it burn. This symbolized that his energy was washed from us by the water, our circle purified by fire, and that the womb of the great mother, symbolized by the cauldron, was rebirthing our group anew.

The unlit white candles were taken to all four cardinal points and the points in between. White is the color of protection. We blessed and lit them to fortify our circle's energy, to protect us from all negative intent from Bad-Witch that might be directed our way.

Next, we each took a length of the black yarn, a color that can absorb energy. We tied the yarn around our foreheads and sat down to get comfortable. I guided the group down into a deep, altered state of consciousness. Each person then engaged in a magickal trick known as time manipulation. Witches know that all time is now—there really is no past or future, only one great present. Each coven member went back, in his or her own way, and mentally restructured his or her first meeting with BadWitch as if it had never taken place. We repeated the newly created events over and over in our minds until they became as real as possible, attempting to erase BadWitch from our memories.

When we finished, we took the pieces of black yarn, which had absorbed these unwanted memories, and burned them, thus freeing our group mind from his influence.

I then pronounced the words of banishment:

Be it known that from this time forward the one called in this incarnation by the name BadWitch is known to us no more. His image shall never again be recalled, his face never seen, his voice never heard, and his name never uttered in this sacred place. In the name of the Lord and Lady, and in the name of earth and air, and fire and water which stand guard at this sacred circle, banished be he. So Mote It Be!

After a banishment it is a good idea to stay together as a group for a while. Go out for coffee, see a movie, take a walk. Just do something so that you take your minds off the event. This is will help forge your new bonds and strengthen your fresh start together.

When a Beloved Member
Must Leave the Coven

Sometimes individuals leave a coven for reasons that have nothing to do with dissatisfaction in the group. Often the reasons are beyond his/her control, such as having to move away from the area due to job demands.

Sometimes people have been splitting time between two covens, and now finds that only one is practical for them to manage at this time. At other times, members will move on to a coven that practices a specific tradition in which they are interested. In most of these cases, the members carry away only good feelings about their coven experience. They may even keep in touch with one another as good friends who are parted tend to do. It is certain that these folks will carry their positive experiences (read positive energy) into the dynamics of the next group in which they work.

When a single member of the group must leave, or chooses to leave, it is nice to mark the occasion with a special ritual. Ideas to include are:

- Have everyone take turns sharing aloud special memories about the coven, particularly events in which this person was involved.
- Invite any former students of the person to a big farewell party.
- Make a keepsake book in which you place all your addresses, and maybe some photos.

- Create a special blessing for the person and/or his or her family if they are moving away. Perhaps you can prepare a safe travel amulet, or a talisman to help them find compatible Witches in their new hometown.

Closing a Coven on Good Terms

Clan Eireannach came to an end when more than half of the members had to move from the the area, and the woman who was the driving force behind our coven became seriously ill. Other covens will simply fade away because people move to other cities, take on new obligations within their families, take jobs that leave them little time for the commitment to the coven, go away to school, or have to move due to military service.

If the coven as a whole must part, a ritual to close down the energies you so painstakingly built is not just nice—it is a good idea. You want to sever those group mind ties so that each of you is fresh and able to go on to new group experiences with an open mind. Try any of the following:

- Spend some time in your circle reminiscing about the fun you've had, the spells that succeeded and failed, the students you saw pass through your group, et cetera.

- Run an orange (for friendship) or blue (for loyalty) ribbon around the perimeter of the circle, then have each person cut a piece as a keepsake. You may even want to bring along a laundry marker or other indelible pen so you can all sign each other's piece of ribbon.

- Put together a coven memory book that you copy and pass out to each other. Be sure to include everyone's address and phone number so that you can keep in touch.

- Bury or burn an item that belonged to the coven as a whole. This might be the coven compact, an altar cloth, or some other item that is infused with your collective energy. This symbolizes that the group energy has come to an end.

AFTERWORD

ONE OF MY BEST FRIENDS once described coven life as "a joyful chaos." She wasn't far wrong. When you are part of a coven you always have a built-in source of love and support—and guaranteed headaches. As in any worthwhile relationship, you learn to take the downs with the ups, and keep on loving just the same. Most Witches who have been in good covens would not trade the experience for anything in this world or the next.

The information and stories about coven work presented in this book come largely from my own experience, or from that of close friends, and cannot hope to be inclusive of all the many differences in interpretation and practice found from tradition to tradition and coven to coven. I do believe that my experiences with covens are typical, in that I have seen the good and the bad, the funny and the ugly. The common elements on which covens base their practices, that are an innate part of the religion known as Witchcraft, remain in place no matter the tradition or coven in which one works. If you belong to, or later join, a coven whose practices are different than those presented here, it is not because they are wrong and I was right, or they are right and I was wrong. Different practices are merely variations on the same theme. As long as the practices are positive and meaningful, their inherent worth need not be questioned.

As I complete this manuscript, I mark my fifth year as a solitary Witch, if there truly is such a creature. I believe that anyone connected with the larger Craft community in any way is never really alone. I live under the same roof with someone who shares my spiritual beliefs and practices, and I have friends—both new and old—on whom I can rely for support when the Witchy life gets tough. These five years have been an enlightening period of renewal and recharge, change and growth; time that has allowed me to rethink every aspect of my life in the Craft, and has taken me to three different states before bringing me home again, giving me the chance to meet and work with lots of Witches from a variety of backgrounds and traditions.

Having enjoyed the heady experience of a solid, working coven, I know I will not stay a solitary forever, and I hope to return to group work again in the not-too-distant future. In fact, after a few false starts, it looks as if this event will occur sooner rather than later.

The choices of when, where, and how to connect with others are yours to make, and none of them have to be forever choices. They should, and probably will, grow and change as you grow and change. Many terrific Witches and Pagans are out there waiting to know you. What happens after that is up to you.

Whether you choose to live your spiritual life as a solitary, or whether you are already a part of a coven or are seeking a coven right now, I sincerely hope you find everything your heart desires.

Blessed Be!
E. M.

APPENDIX

A Networking Directory

Every attempt has been made to make this list as accurate and up-to-date as possible. However, keep in mind that addresses can change, businesses can fail, and periodicals can cease publication. Please remember to enclose a SASE (self-addressed stamped envelope) whenever making inquiries within your own country, or an IRC (international reply coupon) when querying elsewhere. This is a matter of courtesy, since most Pagan organizations are non-profit, staffed solely with unpaid volunteers, and operate on a very tight budget. Some even have instituted polices of no SASE, no response.

(Please note: if you are reading this book more than a year after the date of publication, it may be wise to confirm prices before sending a check.)

Pagan Periodicals

National/international Craft periodicals can be a surprisingly good sources for local networking. The personals/contacts columns often list addresses of people who are looking for pen pals or local contacts, publish notices of open circles and Pagan gatherings, announce the formation of new covens and study circles, and give addresses for local umbrella organizations that can help you meet people in your area who share your Craft orientation or interest.

The Cauldron
Caemorgan Cottage
Caemorgan Rd.
Cardigan, Dyfed
SA43 1QU, Wales

Send one IRC for updated subscription information on this quarterly, which covers many nature spirituality paths.

Circle Network News
P.O. Box 219
Mt. Horeb, WI 53572

This quarterly publication is the perfect journal for any novice wishing to explore many different aspects of Paganism in a non-confrontational format. A one-year subscription is $15 by bulk mail to U.S.A. addresses; $20 first class to

U.S.A., Canadian, and Mexican addresses; and $27 else-where. Payment must be in U.S. funds. Write for other sub-scription information, or to request a sample copy, currently priced at $5.

Coming Out Pagan
P.O. Box 12842
Tucson, AZ 85732-2942

A quarterly journal for gay and lesbian Pagans. Yearly sub-scription $13 U.S.A., $17 Canada.

The Enchanting News
P.O. Box 145
Marion, CT 06444

Journal of Paganism with a strong focus on networking and activities in the American northeast.

Hidden Path
C/o Windwalker
P.O. Box 934
Kenosha, WI 53141

A quarterly journal of Gardnerian Wicca. Send SASE for rate information.

Green Egg
P.O. Box 1542
Ukiah, CA 95482

Contains beautiful artwork and informative articles. Very professionally produced and widely read. Subscriptions to this quarterly are $15 U.S.A., $21 Canada. Write for other subscription information. Sample copy, $4.95.

Hecate's Loom
Box 5206, Station B
Victoria, BC
Canada V8R 6N4

A quarterly journal, professionally formatted. Yearly rates are $18 U.S.A., $15 Canada. Offers sliding scale rates. Write for other information.

Hole in the Stone Journal
High Plains Church of Wicca
2125 W. Evans #286
Denver, CO 78023

Professionally produced quarterly focusing on the central Rocky Mountain area. $12 U.S.A., $17 Canada.

New Moon Rising
12345 S.E. Fuller Rd., #119
Milwaukie, OR 97222

A quarterly focusing on all aspects of Paganism and magick. $14 U.S.A., $21 elsewhere.

Our Pagan Times
P.O. Box 1471
Madison Square Station
New York, NY 10159

A journal for the magickal folk in the greater New York City area. Twelve issues, $18 U.S.A..

Yggdrasil
C/o Freya's Folk
537 Jones St. #165
San Francisco, CA 94102

A quarterly journal for those interested in Norse traditions. Subscriptions are currently $6 U.S.A. and Canada, $8 elsewhere. Sample issue is $2. Checks are to be made payable to Freya's Folk.

National and International Pagan Organizations

Aside from the large organizations listed below, many regions have smaller organizations that provide support, networking, and a sense of community. Please look in the pages of Pagan publications for these addresses.

Covenant of the Goddess
Box 1226
Berkeley, CA 94704

An international Pagan organization. Very active in politics and ecumenical work. Query for membership information. Members receive COG's excellent newsletter with dues. Send SASE for more information or, if you are on the Internet, check out their home page.

The Fellowship of Isis
Clonegal Castle
Enniscorthy,, County Wexford, Ireland

An international organization of Goddess worshipers with more than 10,000 members. Send one SASE or two IRCs for response.

International Wiccan/Pagan Press Alliance
P.O. Box 1392
Mechanicsburg, PA 17055

Membership in the WPPA is open to all, not just writers and publishers. Current annual rates are $18 U.S.A., $20 Canada, and $27 elsewhere. The biannual newsletter, *The Midnight Drive,* discusses trends and news from the Pagan publishing industry, keeps you abreast of the current state of legal problems and other issues facing the Pagan community, and provides ordering information for books from small presses that are hard to find elsewhere.

Pagan Education Network (PEN)
P.O. Box 1364
Bloomington, IN 47402-1364

Organizes Pagans on the local level to shape politics in favor of religious freedom, and to disseminate correct information about Wicca/Paganism. Information and sample newsletter, $3.

The Pagan Federation
BM Box 7097
London WC1N 3XX
England

Founded in 1971, this British-based organization seeks to make itself a forum for all European Pagan traditions, and to promote understanding, networking, and exchange of ideas between them. Send one SASE or two IRCs for membership information.

Pagan Spirit Alliance and **Lady Liberty League**
℅ Circle Sanctuary
Box 219
Mt. Horeb, WI 53572

For membership application to PSA, send SASE to Circle. LLL involves itself in aiding Pagans who face legal difficulties due to their religion.

Witches' Anti-Defamation League
℅ Black Forest Publishing
P.O. Box 1392
Mechanicsburg, PA 17055

Modeled on the very effective Jewish Anti-Defamation League, this group actively combats discrimination against persons involved in nature religions. Include SASE for response.

Witches' League for Public Awareness
P.O. Box 8736
Salem, MA 01970

This organization seeks to educate the public about nature religions, and tackles discrimination issues. Include a business-sized SASE for response.

Witches Today
Box 221
Levittown, PA 19059

An organization whose goals are helping to educate the general public about Witchcraft and Paganism, and maintaining religious freedom for everyone. If you are interested in aiding their efforts on the local level, please write with SASE.

Organizations that Foster Pagan Contacts

World Pagan Network
℅ Chris West
721 N. Hancock Ave.
Colorado Springs, CO 80903
e-mail: ceile@aol.com

This network is staffed by volunteers (and always looking for others!) from all over the place who attempt to locate local contacts for those who request them. At present there is no charge for this service. Please include a detailed description of the area in which you are searching. If you would like to be listed as a contact person or organization in your area, let them know. Send SASE or IRC to ensure response.

Covenant of Unitarian Universalist Pagans (CUUPs)
P.O. Box 442
Boyes Hot Springs, CA 95416
(707) 939-7559
e-mail: CUPPs@aol.com

Organization with a growing following in the United States. It works with Unitarian Universalist Churches to give Pagans a safe place to meet, network, and gain tax-exempt status as a legally recognized "church."

Books About or Containing Information on Wiccan/Pagan Group Dynamics and Contacts

Buckland's Complete Book of Witchcraft by Raymond Buckland. Llewellyn Publications, 1986. Final chapter contains an overview of some of the major Craft traditions and how to contact their parent organizations.

Circle Guide to Pagan Groups by Circle Sanctuary. First published in 1970, and updated at intervals ever since. If you have a Pagan gathering place, occult store, open circle, et cetera, please ask about being listed in their next edition. Write with SASE to Circle Sanctuary/ P.O. Box 219/ Mt. Horeb, WI/ 53572 for current price, or see a recent copy of "Circle Network News."

Circle Network News, Summer 1986: "Group Dynamics." See address under "Periodicals." Back issues are still available at $3.50, postage paid (payment must be in U.S. funds). Be sure to request the issue by name, "Group Dynamics," and by date, Summer 1986.

Creating Circles of Magic and Power by Caitlin Libera, Crossing Press, 1994. Charts the story of the growth of an all-women coven and shows how they dealt with internal difficulties.

The Phoenix from the Flame by Vivianne Crowley, Aquarian Press, 1994. Chapter 14 ("Becoming a Pagan") contains some good networking tips, and the appendix ("Pagan Resources Guide") lists lots of organizations, magazines, and publishers.

Positive Magic (revised edition) by Marion Weinstein. Phoenix Publishing Co., 1981. Chapter 9 ("Widening the Circle") discusses group dynamics.

To Ride a Silver Broomstick by Silver RavenWolf. Llewellyn Publications, 1993. Chapter 14 ("Webweaving") presents ideas for making Craft contacts.

Wiccan Resources: A Guide to the Witchcraft Community by Michael Thorn, 1992. Write for current price with SASE. Address to Michael Thorn/P.O. Box 408/ Shirley, NY 11967-0408.

Making Techno-Pagan Contacts

More than thirty million computers around the globe are currently hooked up to the Internet, dubbed the "information superhighway." On the Net are hundreds of Wiccan/Pagan resources ranging from web sites to newsgroups and from chat rooms to local bulletin boards. Some modern Witches—calling themselves Techno-Pagans—are even using the net to hold rituals. Listing any of these sites here would probably be pointless since things tend to come and go quickly in cyberspace, but you need to be aware that these sources are out there. Check with your local computer stores for the numbers of local bulletin boards. For other sites, use the search engine commands built into your system by keywording Pagan, Wicca, and/or Witchcraft.

Books for Learning More about Basic Witchcraft

Buckland, Raymond. *Buckland's Complete Book of Witchcraft* (St. Paul: Llewellyn, 1986); *Witchcraft from the Inside*, 3rd ed. (St. Paul: Llewellyn, 1995).

Cabot, Laurie. *The Power of the Witch* (New York: Delta, 1989).

Crowley, Vivianne. *The Phoenix from the Flame* (England: Aquarian Press, 1994).

Cunningham, Scott. *The Truth About Witchcraft Today* (St. Paul: Llewellyn, 1988); *Wicca: A Guide For the Solitary Practitioner* (St. Paul: Llewellyn, 1988).

Leek, Sybil. *The Complete Art of Witchcraft* (New York: Signet, 1971).

RavenWolf, Silver. *To Ride A Silver Broomstick: New Generation Witchcraft* (St. Paul: Llewellyn, 1993).

INDEX

Clan Eirannach's basic healing ritual, 128–129

hierarchical (traditions), 11–12, 15, 71, 173

hierarchy, 6, 22, 53, 163

I

Imbolg, 139–140

initiation (*see also* self-initiation), 2, 9, 12, 14, 58, 68, 73, 79–85, 132, 137, 156, 158–161, 163–164, 167

Clan Eirannach's initiation rite, 88–101

inner circle(s), 19, 71, 101, 157–159, 162–163, 165, 167

Internet, the, 36, 55

J

Jewitchery, 33

L

Lammas/Lughnasadh, 139–140

leadership/leaders, 11–14, 22, 41, 45–46, 53, 55, 57, 59, 61, 66, 71, 73, 81, 89, 92, 105, 122, 128, 137, 153, 165, 172, 176–177

Litha, 139

M

Mabon, 140

magick, 9, 15, 30, 56, 61, 67, 72, 101, 106, 113, 115–125, 127, 138, 140, 143, 153–154, 159, 162, 169–170, 177

"must-haves" list, 22–25, 53, 61

N

networking, 5–7, 16, 18, 27–35, 37–39, 41, 43, 45–47, 49, 53, 57–58, 61, 63, 66, 145–147, 149, 151–153, 162, 173

S

sabbat, 140

Samhain, 113, 139–142, 149

Saunders, Alexander, 15

scourge, 83

secrets, 8, 58, 61–62, 84, 86–87, 92, 97–98, 101, 104, 155, 167–170

self-initiation, 2, 5, 14, 23, 58, 73, 160

skyclad, 16–17, 53, 82, 105, 163

solitary (solitaries), 6–7, 27, 33, 59, 63, 88, 118–120, 143, 160, 178

substance(s) (use in coven), 17–18, 41, 73, 179

T

teaching, 67, 155–160, 165–167

those you shouldn't teach, 165–167

teaching covens, 7, 18, 37, 66, 71, 155,

159–162

Clan Eirannach's teaching chart, 160–161

teachings, 8, 96, 103, 116, 162, 169–170

Threefold Law, 98, 116, 180

W

Wicca(n), 6–7, 9, 15, 31, 33, 36, 40, 47, 56–57, 62–64, 69–70, 85, 88–89, 91, 98, 101, 127, 131–132, 141, 143, 156, 161–162, 164, 166–167

Witch war(s), 145, 152–154

Witta(n), 37, 88, 90, 92, 96–97, 100–101, 140, 142, 156, 160–162

Y

Yule, 139

☾ ORDER LLEWELLYN BOOKS TODAY!

Llewellyn publishes hundreds of books on your favorite
subjects! To get these exciting books, including the ones on the following
pages, check your local bookstore or order them directly from Llewellyn.

Order Online:
Visit our website at www.llewellyn.com, select your books, and order
them on our secure server.

Order by Phone:
- Call toll-free within the U.S. at 1-877-NEW-WRLD (1-877-639-9753). Call toll-free within Canada at 1-866-NEW-WRLD (1-866-639-9753)
- We accept VISA, MasterCard, and American Express

Order by Mail:
Send the full price of your order (MN residents add 7% sales tax) in
U.S. funds, plus postage & handling to:
> **Llewellyn Worldwide**
> **P.O. Box 64383, Dept. 0-7387-0294-3**
> **St. Paul, MN 55164-0383, U.S.A.**

Postage & Handling:
> **Standard** (U.S., Mexico, & Canada). If your order is:
> > Up to $25.00, add $3.50
> > $25.01 - $48.99, add $4.00
> > $49.00 and over, FREE STANDARD SHIPPING
> (Continental U.S. orders ship UPS. AK, HI, PR, & P.O. Boxes
> ship USPS 1st class. Mex. & Can. ship PMB.)

> ### International Orders:
> **Surface Mail:** For orders of $20.00 or less, add $5 plus
> $1 per item ordered. For orders of $20.01 and over, add
> $6 plus $1 per item ordered.

> ### Air Mail:
> *Books:* Postage & Handling is equal to the total retail
> price of all books in the order.
> *Non-book items:* Add $5 for each item.

*Orders are processed within 2 business days. Please allow for normal
shipping time. Postage and handling rates subject to change.*

Celtic Myth & Magick
Harness the Power of the Gods & Goddesses
Edain McCoy

Tap into the mythic power of the Celtic goddesses, gods, heroes and heroines to aid your spiritual quests and magickal goals. *Celtic Myth & Magick* explains how to use creative ritual and pathworking to align yourself with the energy of these archetypes, whose potent images live deep within your psyche.

Celtic Myth & Magick begins with an overview of 49 different types of Celtic Paganism followed today, then gives specific instructions for evoking and invoking the energy of the Celtic pantheon to channel it toward magickal and spiritual goals and into esbat, sabbat and life transition rituals. Three detailed pathworking texts will take you on an inner journey where you'll join forces with the archetypal images of Cuchulain, Queen Maeve, and Merlin the Magician to bring their energies directly into your life. The last half of the book clearly details the energies of over 300 Celtic deities and mythic figures so you can evoke or invoke the appropriate deity to attain a specific goal.

This inspiring, well-researched book will help solitary Pagans who seek to expand the boundaries of their practice to form working partnerships with the divine.

1-56718-661-0

464 pp., 7 x 10, softcover   **$19.95**

Magick & Rituals
of the Moon

Edain McCoy

(Formerly titled Lady of the Night)

Harness the energy of "Lady Luna." Moon-centered ritual,
a deeply woven thread in Pagan culture, is often confined
to celebration of the full moon. Edain McCoy revitalizes
the full potential of the lunar mysteries in this exclusive
guide for Pagans.

Magick & Rituals of the Moon explores the lore, rituals,
and unique magickal potential associated with all phases of
the moon: full, waxing, waning, moonrise/moonset and
dark/new. Combined with an in-depth look at moon magick
and rituals, this book offers a complete system for riding the
tides of lunar magick.

Written for both solitary and group practice, Magick &
Rituals of the Moon breaks new ground by showing how
both men and women can Draw Down the Moon for
enhanced spirituality. Pagans will find fun and spirited suggestions on how to make the mystery of the moon accessible
to non-Pagans through creative party planning and popular
folklore.

0-7387-0092-4
240 pp., 7 x 10, illus., softcover **$14.95**

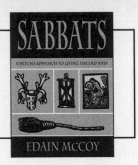

Sabbats
A Witch's Approach to Living the Old Ways
Edain McCoy

Sabbats offers many fresh, exciting ways to deepen your connection to the turning of the Wheel of the Year. This tremendously practical guide to Pagan solar festivals does more than teach you about the "old ways"—you will learn workable ideas for combining old customs with new expressions of those beliefs that will be congruent with your lifestyle and tradition.

Sabbats begins with background on Paganism (tenets, teachings, and tools) and origins of the eight Sabbats, followed by comprehensive chapters on each Sabbat. These pages are full of ideas for inexpensive seasonal parties in which Pagans and non-Pagans alike can participate, as well as numerous craft ideas and recipes to enrich your celebrations. The last section provides 16 complete texts of Sabbat rituals—for both covens and solitaries—with detailed guidelines for adapting rituals to specific traditions or individual tastes. Includes an extensive reference section with a resources guide, bibliography, musical scores for rituals, and more.

This book may contain the most practical advice ever for incorporating the old ways into your Pagan lifestyle!

1-56718-663-7
320 pp., 7 x 10, illus., photos, softcover   **$14.95**

Spellworking for Covens
Magick for Two or More
Edain McCoy

Multiply the power! Here's the only book about magick for covens.

While there are numerous books about creating rituals for group use, and others on how to form, organize, and operate covens, this is the first to discuss working magic in a group (of two or more people). *Spellworking for Covens* addresses raising and sending energy as a group, the power of the group mind, traditional ritual structure, and several types of spells.

- To make it even more practical, this book also provides a grimoire containing texts and instructions for actual spells that can be worked within the group setting.
- The first book to outline the nuts and bolts of creating and executing spells within group settings
- For intermediate-level practitioners and group leaders
- Contains a grimoire with sample spells for coven use
- Written by a practicing Witch and popular author of fourteen books

0-7387-0261-7   **$14.95**
7½ x 9⅛, 264 pp., appendices, bibliog., index

To Ride A Silver Broomstick

New Generation Witchcraft

Silver RavenWolf

Throughout the world there is a new generation of Witches —people practicing or wishing to practice the craft on their own, without an in-the-flesh magickal support group. *To Ride a Silver Broomstick* speaks to those people, presenting them with both the science and religion of Witchcraft, allowing them to become active participants while growing at their own pace. It is ideal for anyone: male or female, young or old, those familiar with Witchcraft, and those totally new to the subject and unsure of how to get started.

Full of the author's warmth, humor and personal anecdotes, *To Ride a Silver Broomstick* leads you step-by-step through the various lessons with exercises and journal writing assignments. This is the complete Witchcraft 101, teaching you to celebrate the Sabbats, deal with coming out of the broom closet, choose a magickal name, visualize the Goddess and God, meditate, design a sacred space, acquire magickal tools, design and perform rituals, network, spell cast, perform color and candle magick, divination, healing, telepathy, psychometry, astral projection, and much, much more.

0-87542-791-X
320 pp., 7 x 10, illus., softcover   **$14.95**

Wicca
A Guide for the Solitary Practitioner
Scott Cunningham

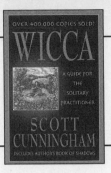

Wicca is a book of life, and how to live magically, spiritually, and wholly attuned with Nature. It is a book of sense and common sense, not only about Magick, but about religion and one of the most critical issues of today: how to achieve the much needed and wholesome relationship with our Earth. Cunningham presents Wicca as it is today: a gentle, Earth-oriented religion dedicated to the Goddess and God. This book fulfills a need for a practical guide to solitary Wicca—a need which no previous book has fulfilled.

Here is a positive, practical introduction to the religion of Wicca, designed so that any interested person can learn to practice the religion alone, anywhere in the world. It presents Wicca honestly and clearly, without the pseudo-history that permeates other books. It shows that Wicca is a vital, satisfying part of twentieth century life.

This book presents the theory and practice of Wicca from an individual's perspective. The section on the Standing Stones Book of Shadows contains solitary rituals for the Esbats and Sabbats. This book, based on the author's nearly two decades of Wiccan practice, presents an eclectic picture of various aspects of this religion. Exercises designed to develop magical proficiency, a self-dedication ritual, herb, crystal and rune magic, recipes for Sabbat feasts, are included in this excellent book.

0–87542–118–0, 240 pp., 6 x 9, illus., softcover $9.95

To order, call 1-877-NEW-WRLD

Prices subject to change without notice.